D0721558

CALGARY PUBLIC LIBRARY

FEB - - 2015

THE ART OF THE JOHN DEERE TRACTOR

LEE KLANCHER

Voyageur Press

To my mother, Diane Stehr, who believes anything is possible.

First published in 2011 by Voyageur Press, an imprint of Quarto Publishing Group USA Inc., 400 First Avenue North, Suite 400, Minneapolis, MN 55401 USA

Text and photography © 2011 Lee Klancher

All rights reserved. With the exception of quoting brief passages for the purposes of review, no part of this publication may be reproduced without prior written permission from the Publisher.

The information in this book is true and complete to the best of our knowledge. All recommendations are made without any guarantee on the part of the author or Publisher, who also disclaims any liability incurred in connection with the use of this data or specific details.

This publication has not been prepared, approved, or licensed by Deere & Company.

We recognize, further, that some words, model names, and designations mentioned herein are the property of the trademark holder. We use them for identification purposes only. This is not an official publication.

Voyageur Press titles are also available at discounts in bulk quantity for industrial or sales-promotional use. For details write to Special Sales Manager at Quarto Publishing Group USA Inc., 400 First Avenue North, Suite 400, Minneapolis, MN 55401 USA.

To find out more about our books, visit us online at www.voyageurpress.com.

ISBN: 978-0-7603-4702-7

The Library of Congress has cataloged the hardcover edition as follows:

Klancher, Lee, 1966–
 The art of the John Deere tractor / Lee Klancher. – 1st ed.
  p. cm.
 Includes bibliographical references and index.
 ISBN 978-0-7603-3949-7 (hb w/ jkt)
1. John Deere tractors–Pictorial works. 2. John Deere tractors–History–20th century. I. Title.
 TL233.6.J64K55 2011
 629.225'2–dc22
                    2010029452

Editor: Dennis Pernu
Design Manager: LeAnn Kuhlmann
Designer: Karl Laun

Printed in China

Front cover: The Model 620 was built through 1958. Not quite as clean as the New Generation machines in the works at the time it was introduced in 1956, the 620 nevertheless bore Henry Dreyfuss' timeless influence, as evidenced in the close-up of this 1956 model.

Frontispiece: The streamlined Model AOS was produced from November 23, 1936, to October 28, 1940, during which time only 900 of the orchard tractors were built. This is a 1938 model. The AOS achieved its short wheelbase by using the front-end frame from the Model AI.

Title pages: This 1960 Model 4010 New Generation is serial number 1000, the first Model 4010 manufactured. Original New Generation designs called for the radiator grilles to be placed on the sides. During testing, airflow proved inadequate and a small front grille was added.

CONTENTS

INTRODUCTION

IN THE EARLY 1890S A FARMER NAMED W. J. JAMIESON HAND-BUILT a self-propelled truck that was powered by a Charter engine he had lying around. The machine was gear-driven and, due to his lack of understanding of how gears worked, it ran backward. He gave up in disgust and sent a letter to the Charter Engine Company suggesting that if they could figure out how to make a contraption like this work, he'd buy one.

They did, and the machine they built was one of the first self-propelled gas farm tractors.

We don't know precisely what drove Jamieson to build his backward-running rig. It may have been an obstinate mule or a string of rainy days that left him working in the barn. We can be pretty sure that he wasn't trying to create art.

The means of the people who built the first successful farm tractors were far greater than those of our man Jamieson. These were people determined to make their mark at a time when technology was changing life in ways we can't even comprehend. The problems we face dealing with the latest OS on an iPhone, for example, are more subtle than the raw challenges encountered by turn-of-the-century innovators. The concept of internal combustion was as exotic to the populace as time travel is to us today.

Those early designers were better educated than Jamieson, but they were no more interested in art. They were figuring out how to adapt brand-new technologies to the problems of powering the farm.

With no set guidelines, three-wheel machines, spindly cultivators, and monstrous beasts of steel emerged from hundreds of companies vying to build a successful replacement for draft horses and oxen. The ad hoc styling applied to these machines was an afterthought, Victorian flourishes that took the form of gold pinstriping or brass trim. With their 15-foot-tall wheels, these 20-ton machines are awe-inspiring but their look is neither elegant nor streamlined.

Only after the Model D appeared in 1920s did Deere and Company begin to develop a look for their tractors. The company employed some of the best engineers of the era. Disciplined men such as Theo Brown carefully penned purposeful and Spartan designs, the visual impressions stolid and unflinching. The early letter series John Deere tractors are much more refined than the pioneering Waterloo Boy, perhaps only because the designs were more logical. The empty spaces between frame rails and components are filled, holding the machines together visually.

In the 1930s the general public, not just design wonks, became enchanted with styled vehicles. Deere hired Henry Dreyfuss to help style their Model A and B tractors. Enlisting the services of Dreyfuss proved one of the savviest moves in company history. Henry Dreyfuss and Associates created some of the century's most iconic designs and had a far-reaching influence on American culture. The partnership, which continues to this day, improved Deere's standing on the showroom floor and in popular culture (and ensured their inclusion in any serious study of industrial design).

Despite the fact that engineers and stylists are an acrimonious match in the best of times, Dreyfuss was a perfect fit for John Deere, as he possessed the intelligence and fastidious nature

> "Industrial design is the art of the twentieth century."
>
> — Stephen Bayley,
> *In Good Shape* (1979)

required to create designs that reflected Deere's company ethics. Though his designs were somewhat predictable, this made them no less elegant than those of celebrated contemporaries such as Raymond Loewy or Brooks Stevens. Horizontal lines and elegant tapers on a block form are unmistakably Dreyfuss—and became definitively Deere.

Dreyfuss' clean, powerful lines denote a company with nothing to hide and with pride in their product. The designer dodged the excess curves of Harley Earl at General Motors and expressed his disdain for the wanton commercialism of Stevens. His designs lived by the ethos that form follows function. Simplicity is an elegance easily overlooked by those who dismiss a machine as an appliance rather than the careful result of decades of deliberate work and study.

A photographic studio is a harsh environment in which to appreciate this. Absent the distractions of a bucolic setting, 20,000 watts of heavily filtered light expose every flaw of the machine. Each poorly thought-out bracket, hastily designed component, or ugly fastener stands out.

The tractors in this book surprised me with their hardiness under the studio lights. The designs reveal themselves, and the machines stand proudly under the attention.

The original-condition machines offer a look at John Deere design that runs deeper, in my mind, than the perfectly restored examples. The cracked rubber of a steering wheel that was turned by a direct descendant of the man who built the first plow is art (to the understanding eye) and history (to all).

Dreyfuss is the man given the most credit for the designs chosen here, but the designs you see on these pages resulted from more than a century of design and evolution, from the work of thousands of men and women striving to create a proper tool for the farmer.

While this is true of any John Deere you find working a field or abandoned on a fence row, the machines on these pages are rare pieces, each worth hundreds of thousands of dollars. They are stored carefully, tended to by a staff, and occasionally displayed at shows. In this way, history is preserved and once utilitarian tools become the treasured property of people with the means to acquire them and the sensibilities to appreciate them.

People travel for days to visit the collection from which these machines were culled. Some merely cross county lines, while others traverse oceans and continents to view the Kellers' machines and, if they are lucky, spend some time listening to Walter and Bruce tell stories about the machines' importance.

So here are objects that have outlived their intended purpose—their only remaining purpose is objectification. The monetary value of these tractors may be spurred by nostalgic collectors, but their cultural currency is equally high. They resulted from millions of man hours logged by some of the world's brightest and best minds.

These objects shaped our lives and helped create the world we live in.

The only word I can find to describe such things is *art*.

The Keller Collection

The machines in this book are all from the Keller collection in Brillion, Wisconsin. The father-and-son team of Walter and Bruce Keller has more than 600 tractors, making theirs one of the world's largest private collections of farm tractors. More than 400 of their tractors are John Deeres.

The Kellers house their collection in seven sheds and one custom-designed brick showroom with glass windows. The buildings are not open to the public, but if you make arrangements with Walter he will give you an informal tour. Walter likes to say his tractors are a blessing, in that they tie up his time and money, which would otherwise be spent on less useful things. His wife reportedly agrees.

The Kellers have a staggering number of machines that were the first or last built, or machines of which only one or two examples were manufactured. As a result, the machines in this book are some of the rarest, most valuable Deere tractors in existence.

Many of the tractors included here have not appeared before in books or in shows. They were selected for inclusion in this book with history in mind, and a number are in original condition, meaning they have never been restored or even repainted.

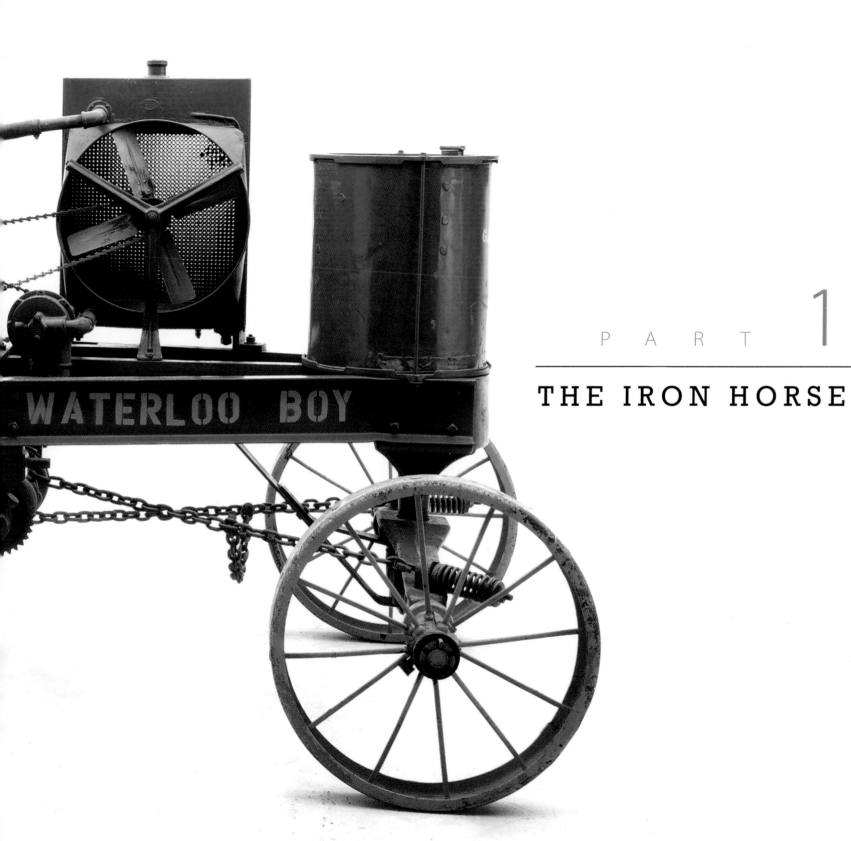

PART 1

THE IRON HORSE

1916 Model R
Waterloo Boy

"The farmer who is buying a tractor . . . does not care much what a tractor looks like or what it consists of, or at present even what its efficiency is. He wants something that will do his work better than a horse."

— C. M. Eaton, *The Farm Tractor*, Society of Automotive Engineers paper (1916)

IN 1892, IOWA INVENTOR JOHN FROELICH built a self-propelled tractor by mounting a Van Duzen engine on a chassis of his own design. Froelich's machine functioned well enough to attract the attention of an investor, and together they founded the Waterloo Gasoline Traction Engine Company in 1893.

Selling tractors at a time when no one really knew what they were was a challenge. Not surprisingly, the company sold only two tractors that year. The company reorganized in 1895 as the Waterloo Gasoline Engine Company. Froelich lost everything but moved on to great wealth inventing the washing machine and air conditioner.

Waterloo Gasoline Engine Company continued to develop a self-propelled machine with the help of Louis W. Witry of Waterloo, Iowa, who fashioned a workable tractor in his backyard shed. That tractor became known as the Waterloo Boy, and was first sold in 1912.

This was a fascinating time for farm tractor development. When the Waterloo Gasoline Traction Engine Company was founded in the 1890s, less than a dozen companies were building and selling tractors. That trend held steady through 1907. Then numbers began to climb as the world slowly realized that the tractor would be the next big development in farm technology. By 1912, 31 companies combined to sell 11,500 tractors. During the next five years, opportunistic engineers, financiers, and shysters jumped into the fray. By 1917, 124 different companies built and sold 62,742 units.

While all this development was taking place, John Deere was selling machines from other makers and developing their own. None of their in-house tractors were sold in volume, however, and the company bought the Waterloo Gasoline Engine Company in 1918 for $2.35 million. Horses still provided most farm power at the time, but more than one million were sent for military use in World War I, and equine prices rose nearly 150 percent. Tractors suddenly became viable options for belt and plowing power on the farm.

In 1918, 142 tractor makers sold an astounding 132,697 tractors in a wide variety of configurations and sizes. Some of the early tractors were all-wheel drive, and others used a large single-drive wheel on Rube Goldberg-esque machines draped in open gears and exposed valves. It was a time of great creativity generated by a problem that no one knew how to solve.

The Waterloo Boy tractors sold well in this environment, with John Deere moving more than 9,000 machines in 1918 alone. The best part of the Waterloo purchase, however, was a design the company kept hidden until the last minute of the sale. The drawing-board discovery would require more than six years of refinement before it could be unveiled, but it was the beginning of a machine that would define John Deere farm tractors for more than 40 years.

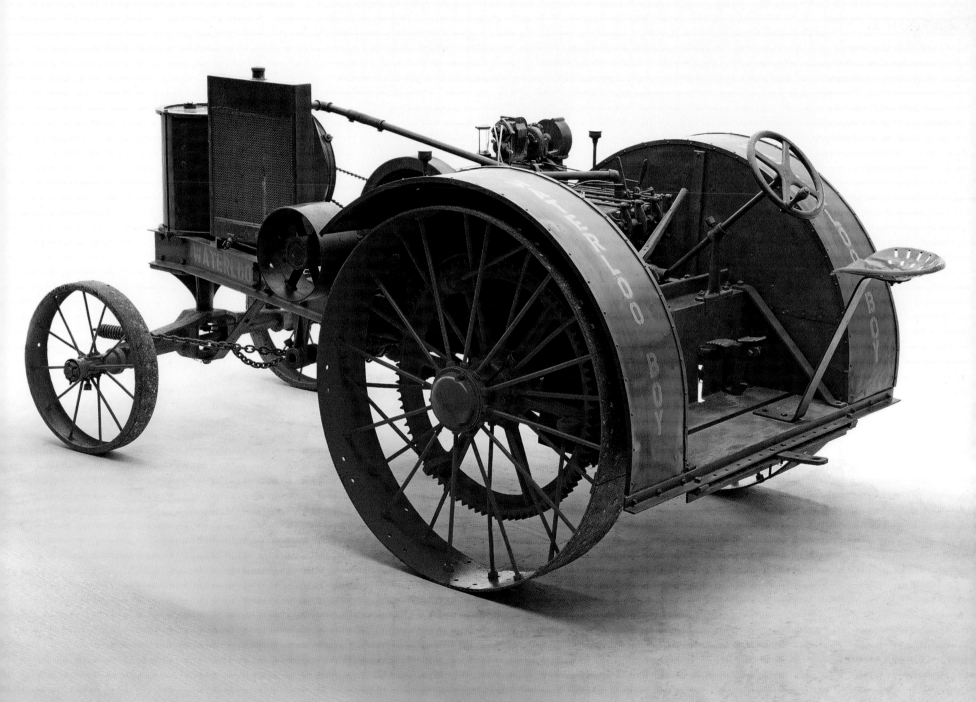

The Waterloo Gasoline Engine Company built several tractor models, beginning with the first Waterloo Boy introduced in 1912. The Model R was built from 1915 to 1919.

Early farm tractor designers were concerned primarily with creating machines powerful enough to be useful, cheap enough to be cost-effective, and reliable enough to last an entire season in the dust and dirt without parts replacement. Designs generally put the fuel tank and radiator in the front (OPPOSITE), with the engine in the rear.

The Model R engine (RIGHT) makes about 12 horsepower at the drawbar, and the machine weighs roughly 6,200 pounds. Top speed is about 2.5 miles per hour. The magneto ignition, gear drive, and radiator were state of the art. This 1916 Model R uses round spoker wheels and a steering system is linked with a chain, which is about as easy to operate as you might expect.

This machine bears serial number 1460. Only about six Model Rs with earlier numbers are known to exist.

1926 Model D

2

"If the form of a machine is stylistically pure, it is because it gives expression to its constructor's conscious intentions and actualizes the plan he has conceived through the most perfect, simple and economically appropriate means."

— Curt Ewald, *Die Form* (1927)

THE ARCHITECTS OF THE MODEL D were steady-handed sorts, not the types to bend to the whims of a tractor-hungry audience. The model's development took place during one of the most dramatic eras in history.

By the time the number of U.S. tractor makers peaked at 186 companies in 1921, Deere & Company had spent three long years working on the design started by the Waterloo Gasoline Engine Company for the Model D.

Between 1918 and 1921, dozens of opportunists rushed in to make farm tractors, but Deere & Company had smartly limited their exposure to the Waterloo Boy Model N and Model R. The machines were a bit staid for the times, and hardly a match for Henry Ford's progressive Fordson or even the more conservative models built by the International Harvester Company (IHC). Despite the fact that Deere sold only 79 tractors in 1921, they did not rush the Model D into production. Experimental models were built, tested, and refined.

Perhaps the impetus for their reluctance was the vicious price war between Ford and International Harvester Company leader Cyrus McCormick, a feud that would change the tide of tractor building from an opportunist's dream to a place where only the strong would survive.

While Ford and IHC exchanged price cuts and traded profits for market share, Deere & Company quietly and economically developed a nicely balanced machine. Its power came from a refined version of the horizontal parallel twin-cylinder used in the Waterloo Boy Model N. Even in the early 1920s, a twin was a bit behind the times. Developing a four-cylinder engine was expensive, though, and Deere decided to save money.

The first production Model D was built as a 1923 model and it dramatically improved upon the Waterloo Boys. While the unit frame and enclosed valvetrain soften and smooth the look, the hood is the key to the machine's handsome visage.

Good looks and a sturdy two-cylinder engine would serve the Model D well. Sales were solid, and Deere kept refining the machine until 1953, making the D the longest-lived model in company history.

Design advances introduced with the Model D included a unit frame, which uses a cast tub rather than frame rails to provide rigidity. However, the long channel between the steering wheel and the curvaceous hood (RIGHT) reveal the D's Waterloo Boy roots—it's still a fair bit of open space that later machines would fill.

(BELOW) The front axle on the first 50 Model D tractors was a fabricated unit prone to breaking. Later models, including this 1926 example, used a cast unit.

This Model D is one of the first machines the John Deere factory painted anything other than green. The reinforced hitch (OPPOSITE) suggests this tractor was intended for industrial work, which makes sense given the orange paint.

(FOLLOWING SPREAD) Kay Brunner cast wheels are another of this tractor's distinctive features.

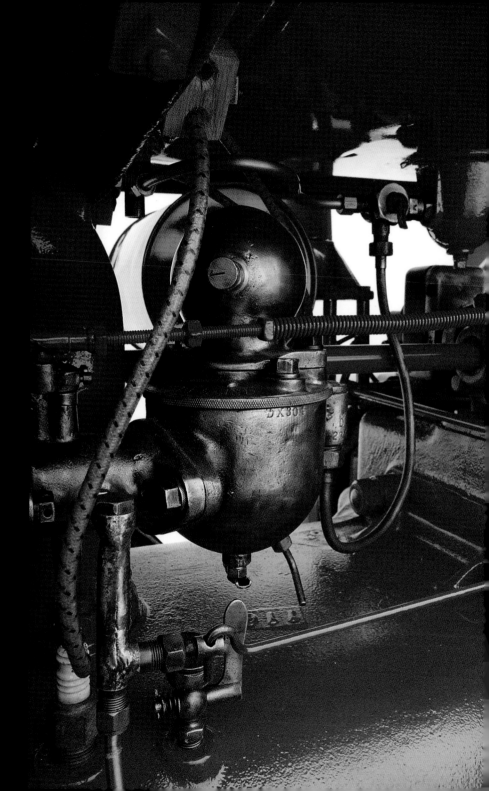

The Model D engine evolved during the machine's long production span. This Model D used a Schebler AD107R carburetor (RIGHT).

(FOLLOWING SPREAD) The earliest Model D tractors used a 26-inch spoked flywheel. Later models, including this 1926 tractor, used a smaller 24-inch version and were known as "spoker Ds."

1928 Model C
Experimental

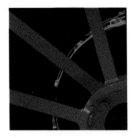

3

"I take art to be a beautiful and original visual solution to a pre-existing problem."

— Stephen Bayley, *In Good Shape* (1979)

THE MODEL D WAS AN UNQUALIFIED SUCCESS, but International's brand-new general purpose Farmall was creating a sensation. Deere needed a competitive machine—quickly.

The team in charge of accomplishing this was led by Theo Brown, one of the company's star engineers. On September 30, 1925, he traveled from Waterloo to Ames, Iowa, to meet with other Deere & Company designers and establish parameters for building a successful machine. On October 5, Brown wrote that he and his team believed the new tractor could use a wide-front design with a cultivator that bolted to the frame, just ahead of the front wheels. On October 16, Brown built a model of the proposed "All-Crop" tractor, and a few days later, the team fastened a crossbar rigged with cultivators to the front of a Fordson. The hand-built unit tested better than expected.

Brown spent December 1 at the factory inspecting a full-scale mockup with Deere & Company President Charles Wiman. "The outfit looks good and the center of gravity not so high as we feared," Brown wrote. "In two weeks they are to send the model over here and we will put on the cultivator. If everything turns out well we hope to have a tractor in the field by May 1st."

Brown spent May 19, 1926, testing the new prototype. Refinement ensued steadily. By August 14, Brown wrote, "Our present design is about right."

As the year wore on, Brown recorded a string of improvements along with all-day meetings spent discussing the merits of various changes. The three-row cultivator was constantly debated, but never rejected. In the spring of 1927, testing continued. Linkages were refined and the radiator was widened.

On February 23, 1928, however, Brown's dissatisfaction with the machine was evident in his journal. "It seems to me that the view is the real problem now," he wrote. A few days later, after testing a tricycle front-end model, he felt progress had been made on the principal problem, but he wasn't entirely satisfied. In a move uncharacteristic for Deere & Company, the machine was sent into production anyway.

The first production Model C appeared on March 15. Its production span was incredibly short, and came to an end on April 20. A few months later, Deere & Company issued a dealer notice stating that the name of the Model C was being changed to Model GP (for "general purpose").

More than 35,000 Model GPs were sold between 1928 and 1935. The experience taught a segmented company the importance of developing tractors and implements in concert. The Model GP had serious flaws—the three-row cultivator never worked well and the engine was underpowered. Wiman expected—and Brown would find—more satisfactory results with future machines.

The Model C was the forerunner to the Model GP, and fewer than 100 were produced between March 15 and April 20, 1928. In 1931, Deere & Company declared Model Cs "experimental." The machines were supposed to be returned to the company, rebuilt, and returned to their owners, but at least one (seen here) survived in original condition.

(PREVIOUS SPREAD) The Model C was developed after the Model D was introduced and was designed to be a bit smaller than the D and capable of cultivating crops, hence the high-arched front bolster.

(ABOVE LEFT) The Model C's cockpit design was ad hoc and utilitarian. Instead of gauges, operators were treated to admonishments regarding oil-level maintenance.

(ABOVE RIGHT) The Model C engine was a twin-cylinder of ill repute. Power output was deemed inadequate. However, one great success developed with the C was the power-lift mechanism (OPPOSITE) that raised the cultivator and other tools. In fact, the Model C was developed in conjunction with an unconventional three-row cultivator. Most cultivators available at the time were designed to work two or four rows, and the three-row model was not widely accepted or well regarded.

PART 2

THE ENGINEERS' ERA

1935 Model AR

4

"The designer of industrial products can only be successful if he is imbued with the conviction that machines . . . are good to look at when the problems involved are properly solved."

— Norman Bel Geddes, *Horizons* (1934)

DEERE & COMPANY NEEDED A PROPER SMALL TRACTOR, one that could work on small farms. The Model GP was not that machine, and the expensive lessons learned during the tractor's evolution made a strong impression on Wiman. He took away an understanding that product development required time and care, with all the proper divisions and leaders giving input to major design decisions.

Small-acreage farms made up the largest part of the American farm market, and Deere needed versatile tractors to work on those farms. The development work for these machines was done as the American economy declined. Deere & Company handled the reduced cash flow with aplomb, remaining steadfast in their determination to take the time necessary to develop the right machines.

Brown laid out his expectations at a February 1931 board meeting. He stressed his concern that the company could not meet its goals without a four-cylinder engine. The cost to develop the engine, however, was deemed too high; the new small tractor would retain a two-cylinder.

Deere's Elmer McCormick began to develop a new tractor coded the GX, and Brown periodically tested (and heartily approved of) the new machine. By the end of 1932, the GX was getting high marks and undergoing extensive cost analysis—the tractor not only had to function, it also had to turn a profit.

The GX passed all tests, and was referred to as the Model AA for a short time before becoming the Model A. Introduced in 1934, the Model A was everything that Wiman and his engineers envisioned. Successful on the sales floor and popular with farmers, the machine proved that long, thoughtful development and engineering resulted in superior products.

In 1934, McCormick proposed a standard-tread version of the Model A. The machine would incorporate a wide front end, a shortened wheelbase, a slightly lower center of gravity, and a host of other minor improvements designed to make it ideal for working fields, industrial settings, and orchards.

The Models AR, AI, and AO resulted, and the first of them—the Model AR—was introduced as a 1935 model. It would undergo a host of improvements and styling changes until it was discontinued in 1953.

The Model A defined John Deere as a company that produced machines of the highest quality even when times were difficult, and set the tone for the company's commitment to exhaustive research and design.

The Model AR was designed by a team of engineers led by Elmer McCormick. The group methodically laid out the parameters for the machine before moving on to sketches, wooden mockups, and prototypes.

(PREVIOUS SPREAD) The engine on this 1935 Model AR is a horizontal two-cylinder with 5.50x6.50 bore and stroke. Later ARs used a larger bore. The carburetor (OPPOSITE BOTTOM) is a Marvel-Schebler DLTX-19, and the model has an all-fuel engine, meaning it can burn low-cost fuels such as distillate and kerosene.

(LEFT) The new standard-tread Model A was advertised in a 1935 brochure showing a leaping deer logo on the hood between "John" and "Deere." According to an article in *Two-Cylinder* magazine, none of the Model ARs were produced with the leaping deer logo. The offset radiator cap at the front of the hood was a distinguishing mark of 1935–1940 ARs. Later models featured a centered cap.

(OPPOSITE TOP and FAR RIGHT) The AR's operator's platform is defined by its mechanical components. Gauge placement in this era of design wasn't quite an afterthought (but it was close), and although style was secondary to function, broad rear fenders do provide a bit of elegance (FOLLOWING SPREAD). The 1950 model would be treated to a Henry Dreyfuss and Associates redesign.

This Model AR is serial number 250000, the first production model built. The machine was initially sent to Deere's engineering department for testing before being shipped to St. Louis, Missouri.

1934 Model B

5

"A thing that is bought and sold has no value unless it contains that which cannot be bought or sold . . . The Priceless Ingredient of every product in the marketplace is the honor and integrity of he who makes it."

— *Journal of Commerce* (July 1931)

THEO BROWN SPENT THE FIRST WEEKS OF 1933 sketching a lift for a new tractor. He wrote that the HX was designed to be 65 percent the size of the forerunner to the Model A, and that they hoped to have prototypes running by mid-April. By early February, Brown had come up with a new swinging drawbar design and a ratcheting engagement for the power lift.

The following October, Brown was testing the Model HX in the field with his implements. He was pleased with the results and pasted a number of photographs of the tractors at work into his journal. On October 30, he added a chart showing the number of patent applications filed by each of the major tractor makers between 1931 and 1933. John Deere had filed more than 234 requests—an amazing 41.5 percent of all requests filed.

Brown's power lift was a sensation. On December 1, 1933, he wrote, "IHC seem to be trying to keep away from the power lift on the Farmall as they must realize that we have the idea so well patented. I'm hoping we will capitalize the power lift and get real business from the monopoly we ought to have with it."

A few weeks later, as drizzle fell outside, the experimental group presented to the chairman. The presentation included Elmer McCormick's conclusions regarding the GX and the HX, now known as the new Model A and B, respectively. After a few days of Christmas parties and "blissful relaxation" with his wife, Brown wrote a few lines about his approach to design: "In thinking ahead as to what the tendency in implement design will follow, it seems as tho it might be wise to go around somewhat and talk to farmers and find out what they think they would like to do with machinery etc that they cant [sic] do now. In visiting I might be able to get some new hunches and develop to a point where we could get patent applications in. Now we are using ideas on which I applied for patents five years ago. It is much better to have others try to copy us than to have to try to copy the other fellow."

This philosophy would mark Brown's work. His creativity was fueled by conversations with men of the day who worked long hours with tractors and implements, and his sketches and thoughts resulted in bits and pieces on most John Deere tractors created between 1918 and 1952. The next time you examine a power lift on a John Deere of this vintage, know that the words of hardworking farmers were catalysts for the steel in your hands.

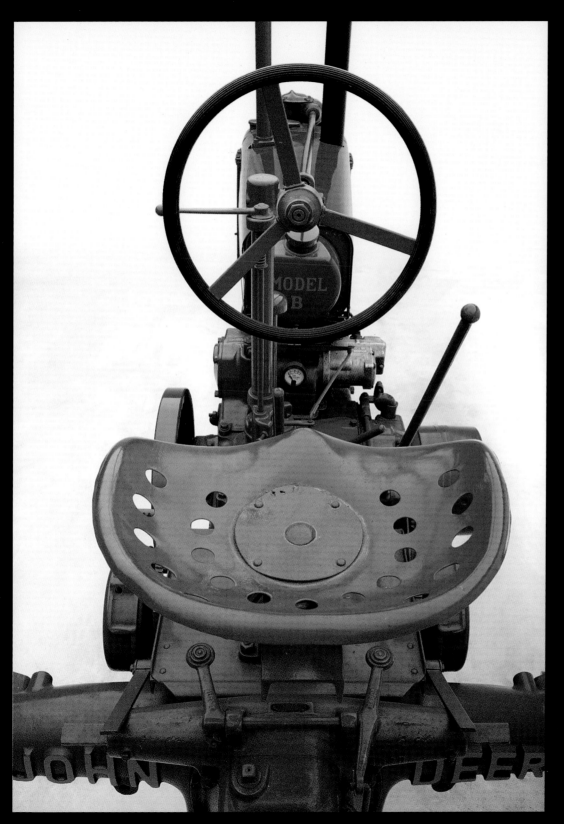

Introduced in 1935, the Model B was a more compact, one-row sibling to the two-row Model A. Elmer McCormick most likely designed the tractor from one of his sketches. The lines are simple and dominated by mechanical components.

(PREVIOUS SPREAD) The hood's leaping deer logo was used on only a very few early Model Bs, and the earliest Bs had the gas tank filler in the center of the tank underneath the steering shaft.

(OPPOSITE) Very early Model Bs used a front pedestal that was attached using only four bolts. As with the gas tank filler, this feature was changed after only a few tractors were produced.

(LEFT) Early farm tractor seats left a lot to be desired, and shifting the four-speed transmission was an awkward operation. Early engineers were more concerned with function than how the machine interacted with the operator.

(ABOVE) More than 300,000 Model Bs were built between 1935 and 1952. This example is the first production model.

1937 Model BI

6

"For many products, design is almost entirely functional, in the sense that either the purposes for which the product is to be used or the technical requirements of the process of manufacture largely control the design."

— Council for Arts and Industry Report (1937)

BY 1936, THE INDUSTRIAL WORLD WAS ENAMORED with design. Styled products such as George Grant Blaisdell's timeless Zippo lighter, Walter Dorwin Teague's Brownie camera, and Henry Dreyfuss' Bell telephone were everywhere.

Men like Harley Earl sketched new designs that would transform automobiles from self-propelled buggies to rolling sculptures. The mechanical exteriors of locomotives were sheathed in sheet metal. Raymond Loewy's buses prowled the streets. The streamlined results became timeless pieces of American culture.

At Deere & Company, engineers like Brown were out in the fields asking farmers how to improve their machines. Opportunists like his colleague McCormick were finding new ways to sell their tractors. One of the potential venues identified was heavy industry.

Tractors with low profiles, high gearing, and attachment points were useful in factories for everything from operating pallet lifts to towing railcars and airplanes and cutting the grass. Such machines had been at work at Deere & Company's own factories for many years. Marketing them to others was only logical.

One of these industrial models was a conversion of the Model B known as the Model BI. The major engineering change was a higher gear ratio in the rear end, which allowed the machine to scoot around the factory or town at a reasonable pace.

Deere & Company built two experimental versions of the Model BI in February 1936, and the first production Model BI arrived a few months later. The machines were typically painted yellow with a few sold in other colors. The Model BI was also sold through Caterpillar dealerships and other industrial equipment outlets. While these partnerships seemed to hold loads of promise, they didn't deliver. The sales goal for the Model BI was 500 units per year—actual production for 1936 was 183 machines.

As the industrial models trickled out the door, Deere & Company executives snapped photographs in the field with Teague's sleek Brownie camera and drove to work in their swoop-fendered Buicks and Chevrolets. The sway that style could hold over the floor managers and corporate buyers who purchased street sweepers and tugs was most likely minimal, but the impact of industrial design on society at large was clear every time someone picked up the phone or stepped out the door.

While most Model BIs were painted yellow, a few were ordered in specialty colors. This 1937 tractor was ordered by the city of Waterloo, Iowa, where it pulled the fire department's ladder truck and was used to mow grass and pump water. The Model BI was produced only between 1936 and 1938. The last production unit was built on April 14, 1938.

(OPPOSITE) The Model BI's front axle is set farther back than on a Model B Standard, shortening the wheelbase. The front end also features pads and tapped holes for mounting equipment, while the low-exiting exhaust is distinct to the industrial model, giving the tractor better clearance for use inside factories and warehouses.

(LEFT and PREVIOUS SPREAD) The BI's seat is a special unit that is adjustable fore and aft.

(FOLLOWING SPREAD) The Model BI features a beefed-up rear axle, with heavier bearings and shafts than those used on the Model B Standard.

1937 Model G
Experimental

7

"The shape of machines is a product of the will of the man who designed them, and not a function of inevitability."

— Stephen Bayley, *In Good Shape* (1979)

AS AMERICA CLIMBED OUT OF THE GREAT DEPRESSION, Deere & Company expanded their line. One addition was a larger sibling to the A and B. Developed as the KX in 1936, the resultant Model G was authorized for production in January 1937.

The machine emerged as an experimental model in May of that year, with 50 units built in the ensuing few months. The tractors were sent out for testing, a few going to Kentucky and Missouri, with most of the rest shipped to Minnesota, Iowa, and Illinois.

In these tests, the Model G engines would run hot enough to burn valves, particularly in southern climes. In response, the engineering department developed and tested a taller radiator. In addition, they redesigned the radiator shutter, fan, and shroud, and even the hood and fuel tank. But the solution proved to require more than additional cooling: The exhaust valves were seated deeper in the head, allowing them to cool better and thus reducing their operating temperature.

Once Deere & Company had the redesign in place, they changed the production models and recalled the roughly 3,000 "low-radiator" models that had been built and sold. Most of these early machines were brought back in for the retrofit, but a few recalcitrant farmers, perhaps working in northern climates that posed no overheating issues, neglected to bring in their machines. Collectors today prize the few remaining low-radiator Model Gs.

Design and development is a constant at any manufacturing company, and Deere & Company was committed to building the best. The company was stalwart with recalls, bringing back their machines to update them with improved engineering. This has resulted in unique survivors— machines that are remarkable today because of quirks of ownership and circumstance.

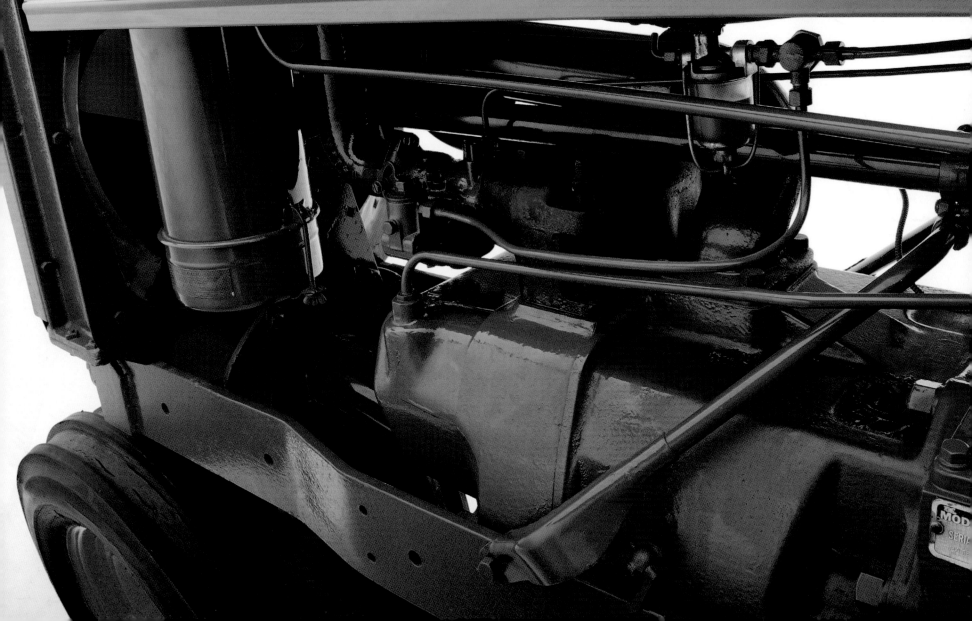

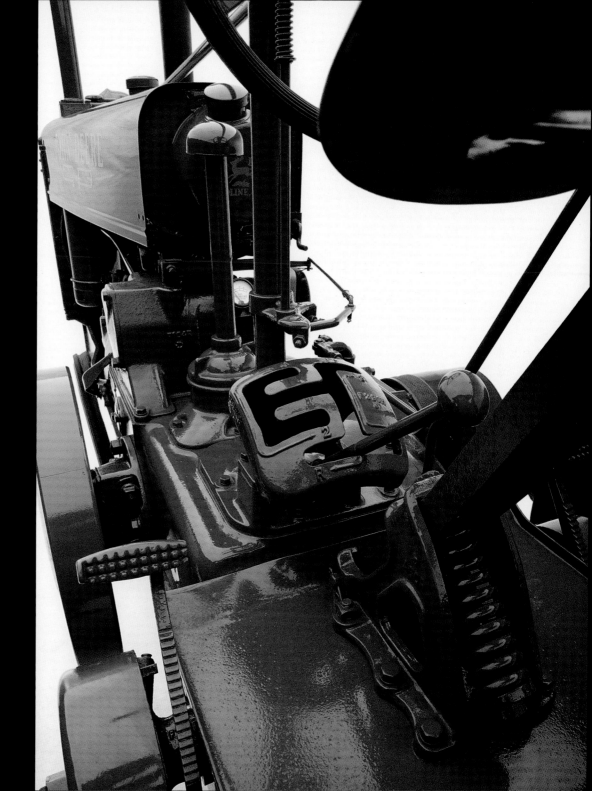

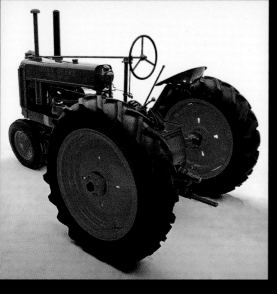

Fifty experimental Model G tractors, including this example, were built in May and June 1937. About 64,000 production units were built from 1938 to 1953.

(PREVIOUS SPREADS and OPPOSITE) The Model G produces 27.6 drawbar horsepower and is equipped with a power lift and 532 rpm power take-off.

This tractor is serial number G1045, the first Model G fitted with an experimental high radiator (OPPOSITE). Model G engines with improved cooling can be recognized by a larger water tube entering the head.

(RIGHT) The early Model Gs feature a four-speed transmission. When the machine was styled, it was treated to an updated six-speed transmission. Rubber tires became standard around the same time.

1937 Model AWH

8

"We need to have a body of men trained in aesthetics and having a sufficient knowledge of technical processes, familiar with the history of visual arts as a whole, and capable of imparting their knowledge and ideas."

— Anthony Bertram, *Design* (1938)

BY 1937, INDUSTRIAL DESIGN had been absorbed into the American psyche. Designers such as Teague, Loewy, and Dreyfuss led high-profile firms that created iconic, saleable American products. Dreyfuss was perhaps best known for his work on the streamlined Hudson J-3a steam locomotives that pulled the New York Central Railroad's *20th Century Limited*.

Some of the Deere & Company engineers at Waterloo Tractor Works eventually convinced Charles Stone, the head of manufacturing, to bring in industrial designers to restyle their tractors. In fall 1937, Stone sent McCormick to New York to speak with Dreyfuss about this idea.

One of Dreyfuss' favorite stories was from his early career, when a movie studio sent him to Sioux City, Iowa, to investigate why their brand-new movie palace there was drawing tiny crowds. Dreyfuss lowered ticket prices, ran triple features, and gave away dish sets, but still found that locals preferred an older theater down the street. He decided to spend three days standing quietly outside the new theater, watching people walk past. Afterward, he had the lush, red carpet in the lobby replaced with a plain rubber mat. Ticket sales exploded. The problem, Dreyfuss discovered, was that local farmers and townspeople hadn't come through the door for fear of dirtying the carpet with their boots.

Dreyfuss, who believed that replacing artifice with function was one of his crowning achievements, proved a good fit for Deere & Company. He accepted McCormick's proposition and went to work with Deere almost immediately. The look of John Deere tractors would never be the same.

Production of the John Deere Model AWH ended with just 27 units, though the tractor is part of the Model A line, of which Deere & Company sold more than 300,000 units from 1934 to 1952.

(PREVIOUS SPREAD) The AWH has an adjustable tread width. The machine's narrow width, combined with a wide tread width, make the model ideal for cultivating vegetable crops. Argentine customers at first felt the beautiful oval-spoked wheels looked too light, when in fact they were stronger than flat-spoked wheels.

(LEFT and ABOVE) The Model A uses a two-cylinder 309-ci all-fuel engine that starts on gasoline and can run on cheaper fuels. The carburetor on this AWH is a Marvel-Schebler DLTX-18. Power is delivered with a four-speed transmission that yields a top speed of 6.25 miles per hour.

A Model A weighs in at about 4,000 pounds and in 1937 cost $1,050—not cheap at the time.

1940 Model BO

9

"Complete adaptation to a humble station in life, perfect fulfillment of a modest destiny, may be far more admirable than meretricious performance in a more exalted role."

— Walter Dorwin Teague, *Design This Day* (1940)

THE LINES OF EARLY JOHN DEERES have a stark, spare beauty to them. These machines were built to serve the farmer, who was applying technology to the world's second-oldest profession at a dizzying rate. As World War I sapped America's workforce, and the nation's increasing population transitioned from rural to urban, farmers were pressed to produce more with less manpower.

By 1940, the tractor had become a useful, reliable tool. Developmentally, the compact and rugged Model B was a light year beyond the Waterloo Boy Model R. Sealed bearings and pressured oiling systems vastly improved durability and longevity, while advances in hitches, lifts, and implements transformed tractor work from a battle to a relative breeze.

Indeed, the farmer had adapted the tool in record numbers. The U.S. Census recorded 246,083 tractors in use on farms in 1920. By 1940, records showed more than 1.5 million tractors in use.

The tractors developed during these two decades—with such advances as four-valve heads, overhead camshafts, and forced induction—set the technological stage for much of what would come over the next 40 years.

The early tractor developers had begun with a nearly blank slate. Their concerns were how to first make a machine that actually functioned, and then rapidly develop and build it for a reasonable price. Appearance was an afterthought for these early pioneers. This changed somewhat in the early 1930s, as engineers like Brown and McCormick penned sketches and built wooden mockups. Their designs have a look that stemmed from an engineer's sense of proportion and balance, the artistic side implicit in their profession.

In the end, however, their designs were concerned much more with function than interaction with human hands or eyes. Only when the machines could perform fundamental tasks did manufacturers use improved appearances and interfaces to distinguish their products. Tractor makers in the middle four decades of the twentieth century evolved their technology, but the major advances of the period were concerned with making the machines better looking and easier to use.

Even as America became embroiled in World War II, Deere & Company tractors continued to work soil at home and abroad. Long before John Deere tractors became collected, hoarded, and sold as rolling works of art treasured for their sound and aesthetics, they fed the world.

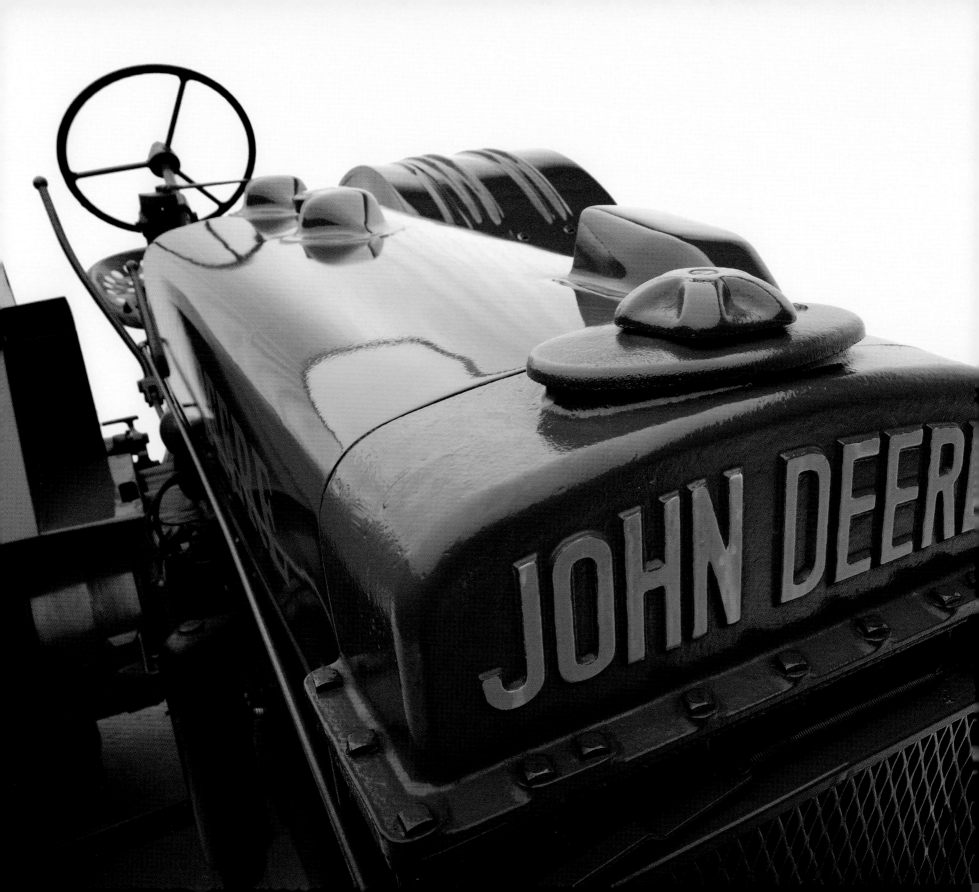

P roduced from 1935 to 1947, the Model BO was equipped with large fenders, an under-slung exhaust, and sculpted coverings over protrusions—all features designed for orchard work. The BO was a modified version of the Model BR, one key difference being differential braking, which allowed the user to make tight turns more easily, another beneficial feature when working an orchard.

(PREVIOUS SPREAD) The engine was originally a 145-ci two-cylinder. The bore was later increased by 0.25 inch to give the machine 175 ci of displacement and some additional horsepower. This 1940 model is equipped with the larger engine, as well as a rare electric-start option. Rubber tires were optional on early Model BOs, but were standard by 1940. Buyers had their choice of cast or spoked wheels.

(OPPOSITE) At 50 inches, the Model BO is a few inches narrower than its linemates, the Model BR and Model BI.

Production of the Model BO averaged 389 per year during its 13-year model life. About 5,000 Model BOs were produced.

PART 3

THE RISE OF STYLE

1938 Model AOS

10

"A good farmer is more interested in the engine of his tractor than the purr of a Cadillac."

— Henry Dreyfuss,
Designing for People (1955)

THE AOS COMES AS CLOSE TO SEXY AS POSSIBLE for a vehicle designed to pull manure spreaders and hay wagons. That curvaceous piece of sheet metal on the flanks has the inglorious job of protecting orchard branches from the tractor's wheels. The appearance suggests streamlining for speed, and one wonders if the AOS wouldn't look more at home at the Indianapolis 500. In fact, Charles Freitag created a painting of an AOS on a banked racetrack, battling with period open-wheel cars, the pilot hammering down the turn wearing a pith helmet as his scarf trails behind him in the breeze.

Created under Elmer McCormick's supervision, the AOS has the most spectacular lines of any tractor in the Deere line in the first half of the twentieth century. It also countered the philosophy of Dreyfuss, who would begin work with Deere & Company in August 1937, long after the AOS was off the drawing boards and into the fields as a test mule. Dreyfuss believed form must follow function, and his design contributions to John Deere would be simple and elegant. Flashy fenders and droop-nose grilles were better suited to Buicks and Buck Rogers films.

The AOS was born when a Deere & Company engineer named Bacon authorized the design on August 7, 1936. The machine would be based on the Model AR, but lowered and streamlined for orchard use. Six experimental machines were built and sent to several test sites around the country. After a year of testing, the experimentals were returned to the John Deere Tractor Works in Waterloo. Two were scrapped, while the other four were rebuilt and sold.

The machines that started as Model ARs and became the prototypes for the Model AOS are distinguished by automotive-type oil dipsticks in the front crankcase on the flywheel side of the engine. The 1937 Model AOS pictured here, one of only two experimental tractors known to exist, was purchased in the mid-1980s at auction.

The Model AOS has a style that was outlandish in its time. It was a statement machine that told the industry that Deere & Company products were more than just implements. The style appeared to resonate with customers in 1937—just over 512 units were sold, a reasonable sale, but production was stopped.

The Model AOS, with its automotive-inspired grille, was produced from November 1936 to October 1940. Only 900 were built and sold.

(PREVIOUS SPREAD and OPPOSITE) The Model AOS is narrow for orchard work. That narrow profile necessitated changes to the clutch assembly, rear-axle housing, crankshaft, and front axle. Deere & Company created the narrow rear end by shortening the Model AR's axle shafts and housing. The drawbar assembly was also redesigned.

In addition, the crankshaft was redesigned, with a new flywheel and other parts helping to shave off another half inch of width. The right main bearing was redesigned, and the crankshaft bearings were rotated 180 degrees.

(RIGHT) The lever for shifting into low gear is bent to provide clearance under the lowered and shortened steering column. The seat is larger and lower than the unit found on the Model AR Standard.

The wheels on this AOS are rare aftermarket models.

1941 Model HNH

11

"If a tractor appears well put together outwardly, it is logical to assume that the internal mechanism is equally sturdy. A dealer, after looking at a new tractor design, once told me, 'If it works as well as it looks, I'll buy it.'"

— Henry Dreyfuss,
Designing for People (1955)

BY THE LATE 1930s, a number of tractor manufacturers were experimenting with streamlining, bright paints, and other styling exercises. Deere & Company raised the bar beyond the previous efforts of in-house engineers when they hired Henry Dreyfuss. His firm turned out to be a perfect fit for the company.

The son of immigrant parents, Dreyfuss was born in New York City and from 1920 to 1922 attended the Ethical Culture Society's private high school. He went on to study stage design under Norman Bel Geddes. Geddes was one of America's first industrial designers, and he taught Dreyfuss how to methodically transform visualizations into physical forms. Working as set designers also taught both men how to create designs that met clients needs and tastes, a key aspect of their success.

By 1925, the 21-year-old Dreyfuss had achieved modest success as a stage designer in New York and determined that his future was as an industrial designer. As the 1930s progressed, Dreyfuss designed corporate airplane interiors for William K. Vanderbilt and others. These dramatic stylings led to coverage in *Architectural Digest* and the assignment to redesign the locomotive and cars for New York Central's *20th Century Limited*, which traveled between New York and Chicago. When the streamlined train debuted in 1936, it was heralded as a breakthrough in railroad design.

In 1937, when Deere & Company sent McCormick to speak with Dreyfuss in New York, the designer was entering a fertile time in his career. In the late fall of 1937, his design firm was tasked with redesigning the Model A and B tractors. The changes suggested by Henry Dreyfuss and Associates (HDA) not only dramatically improved the appearance of the machine, but also enhanced visibility, safety, and the cost-effectiveness of production. Deere & Company had HDA redesign nearly their entire line of tractors, and the "styled" farm tractor was introduced to the market for the 1938 model year.

The tractors sold well and their appearance garnered accolades for decades. Other tractor makers would also turn to well-known industrial designers. International Harvester hired the egotistical genius Raymond Loewy, and Allis-Chalmers employed the sales-minded and sensationalistic Brooks Stevens. Both were great designers, but neither would have meshed with Deere & Company as well as the tidy man known for his elegant style, impeccable ethics, and ever-present brown suit.

The philosophy of functional, simple, and stylish appearance that characterized HDA was a wonderful match for the methodical, research-driven approach of Deere & Company. The partnership forged in New York in 1937 continues on today.

The Model HNH is a narrow version of the Model H, which began development in the fall of 1938. The H was intended to be a row-crop tractor smaller than the Model A, B, or G. The first preproduction Model H was built on October 28, 1938, and shipped to the University of Nebraska for testing. Regular production began on January 18, 1939.

(LEFT TOP) The grilles and hoods of the early styled John Deeres, such as the HNH, bear touches that would come to distinguish Henry Dreyfuss' design aesthetic.

(LEFT BOTTOM) The Model HNH is equipped with a special rear-axle housing that provides additional ground clearance. This design consideration was intended to meet the needs of California row-crop farmers.

(OPPOSITE) Dreyfuss and his team at HDA also brought their design skills to bear on the dashes of styled John Deeres, making them more handsome and easier to read.

Only 37 Model HNH tractors were produced, all between March 11, 1941, and January 23, 1942. One was shipped to Lordsburg, New Mexico; the rest went to dealers and customers in California. This particular HNH, serial number 41760, was built on December 11, 1941, and shipped to Los Angeles.

"Moving away from the perfect, streamlined teardrop forms that dominated industrial design in the early 1930s, Dreyfuss' new approach emphasized an abstract play between vertical and horizontal forms that resulted in a convincing imagery of power."

— Russell Flinchum,
The Man in the Brown Suit (1997)

IN THE LATE 1930s, MANY AMERICAN FARMS were smaller than 100 acres and still relied on animal power rather than tractors. Deer created the Model L to meet the needs of these smallest of farms served by one or two farm animals.

With Brown and McCormick nearly overwhelmed with their design responsibilities, the task of creating this small tractor was shifted to Ira Maxon of the Moline Tractor Division. He brought in former Deere engineer Willard Nordenson to help his thinly funded division create the machine.

Nordenson designed a machine that utilized a short tube-steel frame, a foot-operated clutch, and an outsourced engine. HDA became involved with the project in November 1937. They drew the distinctive lines of the styled Model LA and offered feedback on dozens of details.

In the well-researched account of the Model LA's evolution in his book *John Deere: A History of the Tractor*, Randy Leffingwell writes, "As each new element came under scrutiny, an assortment of paper went by airmail to and from designers and engineers. Seat shape and gear-change lever configurations and the shape of the perforations in hood and grille sheet metal provoked suggestions and alternatives. Dreyfuss' staff and Nordenson's engineers drew and redrew."

One key member of the Dreyfuss staff was Roland Stickney, a highly respected designer best known for his work on the building design for Rockefeller Center and on Duesenberg, Chrysler, and Lincoln automobiles. Stickney transformed the Dreyfuss concept sketches into finished drawings. Many of the sketches done for Deere & Company are credited to Stickney.

The machine created by the engineering efforts of Maxon and the design input of HDA proved timeless. More importantly, the close interaction between the design firm and the engineers would become an integral part of the design process at Deere & Company.

This small tractor evolved from the Model Y that was first built in 1936 and later named the Model 62. In 1938, the machines were again renamed, this time in the Model L series, which remained unstyled until 1938.

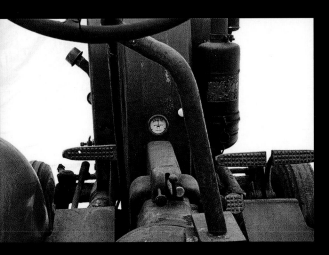

In the Model L series, Deere produced both styled and unstyled Model LIs, introducing the styled version as a 1941 model. The tractor shown here is the first production Model LI. It was shipped to John Deere Harvester Works in Moline and used for various jobs at the plant. Given its lineage, this particular tractor is most definitely *not* a restoration candidate.

(OPENING SPREAD) The styled Model Ls were more distinctly touched by HDA than other tractors from the era. The lines evoke Henry Dreyfuss' iconic Honeywell Chronotherm thermostat. The LI was produced through 1946 and sold for close to $500.

(PREVIOUS SPREAD) The early Model L tractors were powered by a Hercules NXB vertical twin-cylinder gas engine. Later models, including this 1941 tractor, used a 66-ci John Deere vertical twin.

(RIGHT) The Model L seats are offset to make the tractors as short as possible. A shorter tractor was easier to maneuver and to load onto railcars for shipping. Both brake pedals were on the right-hand side (ABOVE). This allowed both to be depressed simultaneously, an innovation that made its way into most John Deere tractors.

1953 Model R

13

"For the Model R Diesel . . .
[Henry Dreyfuss and Associates]
managed to create an image suited
to tremendous power."

— Russell Flinchum,
The Man in the Brown Suit (1997)

THE MODEL R HAD ONE OF THE LONGEST DEVELOPMENT CYCLES of any John Deere tractor. When it was released to the public in 1949, the tractor had spent 14 long years in development and more than 66,000 hours being field-tested.

Large cylinders aren't terribly conducive to diesel ignition. Deere's job would have been much simpler had they been willing to build a four-cylinder diesel engine. They were not. The resulting Model R was the most powerful farm tractor built by Deere & Company up to that time and possibly the most reliable, not to mention one of the best-looking—if your daughter was a farm tractor, you'd want her to date a Model R.

The Model R's design was heavily influenced by Henry Dreyfuss' "form follows function" philosophy. When testing showed that the large cooling fan required to keep the big engine running at the proper temperature gathered debris on the grille, Dreyfuss designed the angle of the grille corrugations so that farmers could easily sweep off the chaff with their hands.

The Model R seen here was sold to Paul Ashauer on June 2, 1953, by Walter Keller's brothers, Reuben and Lester, at the Keller John Deere Dealership in Wisconsin. The tractor was too large to fit on the dealership's truck, so an employee drove the big machine to Ashauer's farm near Menasha.

Ashauer meticulously cared for the R. He kept records for every tire change. He held on to the original factory parts. The tractor still has its original remote cylinder, as well as the drawbar pin sold with it.

By the mid-1980s, Ashauer was done farming. He knew that Walter Keller had started collecting tractors, so he called to see if he was interested in purchasing the machine. Keller agreed. He also drove it back to his museum on the road, just as it had been driven more than 40 years earlier.

An experimental version of the Model R—the Model MX—was first tested in 1941. Another eight years would be spent developing the machine for production. Introduced in 1949 and produced until 1954, the production Model R featured a diesel engine praised for its power and fuel economy.

(OPPOSITE) Development of the diesel engine actually began in 1935. The factory experimented with an engine that started on gasoline and then switched over to diesel. They eventually settled on a design that used a small gasoline-powered pony engine to start the 516-ci twin-cylinder diesel. The engine puts out 45.7 horsepower at the drawbar, up roughly 18 horsepower from the Model D. That power output is coupled with superb fuel economy.

(PREVIOUS SPREAD) The Model R grille was created with input from Henry Dreyfuss and Associates. The distinctive bar splitting the grille on the Model A and Model B was abandoned in favor of a design that was easier to brush off with gloved hands. Pragmatism ruled at HDA, and this innovation earned a patent.

(ABOVE) The Model R uses a five-speed transmission and weighs 7,500 pounds. The operator platform is almost completely covered in sheet metal, with only the controls protruding. The sightlines from the Model R are crisp and clear, with the minimal instrumentation easily visible to the operator.

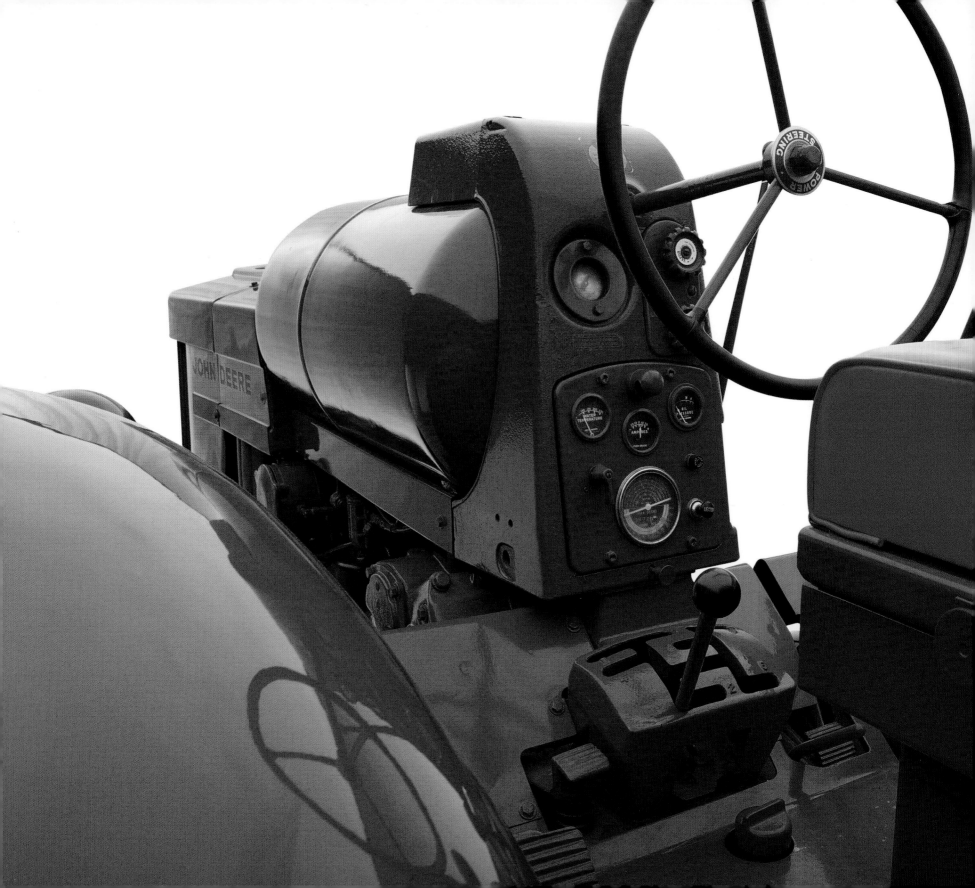

PART 4

THE ART OF REFINEMENT

1953 Model 40
Standard

14

"Our admiration of the antique is not admiration of the old, but of the natural."

— Ralph Waldo Emerson

THE JOHN DEERE MODEL 40 IS A BIT OF A WHITE KNIGHT. Its predecessor, the Model M, was one of Deere & Company's best-selling machines. But that isn't to say it was considered a success.

The Model M was built for the large niche of small farmers looking to add tractors to their operations. Other makers—most notably Ford—were already selling large volumes of such machines. Sales expectations were high for the Model M, and while it sold well, it did not fulfill those expectations adequately enough to please Deere. The M, by corporate standards, was a failure. Brown described the situation in his journal, recording the details of an all-day meeting in November 1950 during which executives concluded the M design was unfriendly to operators (climbing aboard was an ungainly, graceless act) and offered a dearth of equipment.

Designed with improved operator comfort and a wider array of implements and accessories in mind, the Model 40 was brought to market quickly to succeed where the Model M had failed, namely as a direct competitor to the Ford N. The Model 40 filled the bill nicely. While it never seriously challenged Ford, it sold well and worked well.

The tractor photographed here was sold in 1953 by Lolita Tractor in Santa Barbara, California, to Pattie "Tish" Deere Wiman, the wife of John Deere CEO Charles Deere Wiman. The couple kept a winter home in Santa Barbara and bought the tractor to help with maintenance of the estate. Charles died from an embolism on May 12, 1955, and Patti stayed in the home until her death in 1976. Her daughter, Mrs. William Brinton, inherited the property.

The tractor was continuously maintained by the California dealership until 1982, when it was traded in for a John Deere 112 riding tractor. After that, the tractor passed through several collectors before the Kellers purchased it in May 2005. The Model 40 remains in original condition, a weathered but solid piece of history that spent its life working for the Deere family.

The line of tractors that replaced the letter series was designed with input from those who would use them every day. "These new tractors were designed, in a sense, by our farmer customers," said general sales manager Lyle Cherry when he introduced the new line on June 11, 1952.

The Model 40 was available in seven different configurations, including a Hi-Crop, a crawler, and wide and narrow versions. When introduced, the new series offered automatic fuel shut-off valves, a fuel tank designed to allow the machine to run for eight hours without refueling, and an interchangeable front end (PREVIOUS SPREAD).

The cooling system was also upgraded on the Model 40. The longstanding thermosiphon system, which relied on heat to circulate the cooling fluid, was replaced by a pressurized tank system with water pump.

(RIGHT and OPPOSITE) The familiar two-cylinder engine displaced 100 ci and put out 22.9 horsepower at the drawbar, while the new "duplex" carburetor provided better low-end response and fuel economy. The tractor was available with engines that burned gas only or in an all-fuel version that burned low-grade fuels. In 1955, a Model 40 Standard cost $1,521 and came from the factory equipped with a four-speed transmission.

This Model 40 was once owned by Charles Deere Wiman, the great-grandson of John Deere and the man who served as the Deere & Company president from 1928 to 1955. The most critical years of the company were guided by his strong sense of ethics and dedication to research and development.

1956 Model 620
Standard LP

15

"Innovation distinguishes between

a leader and a follower."

— Steve Jobs

THE MID-1950S WERE TURBULENT TIMES at Deere & Company. Long-time company president Charles Wiman passed away in 1955, and the torch of leadership he had carried since 1928 was passed to his son-in-law, Bill Hewitt.

Wiman's dedication to research and development and product excellence, along with his fiscal conservatism, had made Deere & Company the industry's second-place manufacturer behind tractor giant International Harvester. While Wiman's contemporary at IH had buried that company in debt by spending too much capital on developing industrial equipment and appliances, Wiman's approach kept Deere solvent and ready for the next challenge.

Hewitt proved much more aggressive than Wiman. He soon declared his intention to open up the traditionally closed society of Deere management, and brought in high-profile consulting firm Booz Allen Hamilton.

In the fall of 1955, he announced his intention to move the company into the agricultural industry's top position. He took the sales and marketing divisions to task as too passive. He also suggested that the engineering departments were too insular and independent, and stated that the marketing department should have say in design decisions. Along with this, Hewitt called for better interdepartmental communication and mandated more business school education for executives.

With Booz Allen Hamilton's input, Hewitt subtly restructured the company. The old concept of near-complete divisional autonomy was replaced with more centralized management control. The consultant's report suggested the advisory committee, which was mostly a low-stress repository for aging executives, be replaced with one staffed by full-time members from the company's three key divisions: production, sales, and finance. The new committee would be given tremendous knowledge of the company and offer advice to the CEO and other senior executives. The role intended for the committee was fulfilled by the company's long-time senior legal advisor, Edmund Cook, who brought years of experience with the company to his new position.

Hewitt's moves accomplished the nearly impossible goal of decentralizing the design process without destroying the product. At companies such as General Motors in the 1980s and 1990s, design by committee met with disastrous consequences. For John Deere, however, it would prove to be an efficient tack.

In the late 1950s, John Deere introduced the 20 Series with well thought-out upgrades designed to appease customers (and dealers) until the new four-cylinder line was ready. The Model 620 came out in 1956 and was built through 1958. These models were an upgraded and restyled version of the 60 Series. Only 37 Model 620 Standard LPs were built.

(OPENING SPREAD) While not quite as tight and clean as the New Generation machines in the works at the time it was introduced, the 620 has sturdy, timeless lines. The open engine bay offers easy access for service and a more mechanical look than later machines. Shipped to Florida and used in orchards, this particular tractor is equipped with a very rare special-order under-slung exhaust that exits at the rear of the machine. Jim Conner of Henry Dreyfuss and Associates oversaw the addition of yellow paint to the side panels.

(OPPOSITE) The John Deere logo was redesigned for 1956. The deer remained the same, but the tag line "Quality Farm Equipment" was removed, the border's corners were radiused and softened, and the John Deere type became sans serif. The end result was a simpler, more elegant design that signified the company's growing confidence and brand recognition. The Dreyfuss-designed front radiator panels line the bolster, framed by elegantly sculpted fenders.

(RIGHT TOP) The 20 Series features a three-point hitch and Custom Powr-Trol, an improved version of the Powr-Trol attachment system introduced on the Model R. The new system offered load and depth control.

(RIGHT BOTTOM) The Henry Dreyfuss styling influence is apparent in an elegant dash that wraps around the tank and incorporates curves evocative of the Model L.

"Color creates instant impact . . . one's attention is often captured by color before the form or composition is completely distinct."

— Henry Dreyfuss, *Symbol Sourcebook* (1972)

COLOR WAS ALL THE RAGE IN THE 1950s. Eastman Kodak introduced 35mm color film in 1950. Flashy two-color paint schemes emerged on Oldsmobiles and Buicks in 1954, and the rest of the American auto industry followed suit in 1955. At General Motors, designer Harley Earl oversaw a 75-member Styling Color and Interior Design Studio.

A driving philosophy of Detroit design was planned obsolescence. Brooks Stevens claimed to have coined the term. "We make good products, we induce people to buy them, and then next year we deliberately introduce something that will make those old products old fashioned, out of date, *obsolete*," he told *True* magazine in April 1958. "We do that for the soundest reasons: to make money."

Color fit neatly into this paradigm. What simpler way to trump last year's model than rolling out a fresh color?

Henry Dreyfuss was not swayed. "The realistic manufacturer is working towards a fundamental improvement in his product, an improvement that will give the consumer a really convincing reason for trading in the old model," he wrote. "In our fast-changing world, nothing seems so obsolete as the idea of 'planned obsolescence.'" Dreyfuss understood the value of color in communication, but in the Dreyfuss design world, color was simply another element to be wielded carefully.

His firm's major contribution to the John Deere 20 and 30 series was a splash of carefully chosen yellow. The models were thoughtfully refined versions of machines that inspired great pride when introduced by John Deere sales manager Lyle Cherry in 1952. His speech was reprinted in *Two-Cylinder* magazine, published by Lyle's son, Jack: "Never before has any manufacturer presented new tractors with so many outstanding improvements over current models," Cherry stated.

The pride in innovation explains why Deere & Company and Dreyfuss maintained such a long-standing alliance. The 20 and 30 series were elegant, functional machines, the products of more than four decades of innovation.

While the 30 Series kept dealers' doors swinging, Deere & Company's best and brightest were already building the next big thing. Bill Hewitt's new management team left history behind and opened the doors to more outside influence in the design process. Innovation would trump tradition.

Henry Dreyfuss and Associates were involved more closely than ever in the creation of this new line. Some of their suggestions included painting the machines colors other than green and yellow. Color, it seemed, affected even the man in the brown suit.

One key innovation on the 30 Series was the stylish new fenders (PREVIOUS SPREAD and OPPOSITE). In classic Henry Dreyfuss fashion, they provide protection from dirt and an additional margin of safety in case of a rollover.

(LEFT) Evolved from the Model R diesel, the Model 830's engine is a 471.5-ci twin-cylinder diesel. The cylinder bore is just over six inches, and the stroke is eight inches. This Model 830 is equipped with electric start, but the model also could be ordered with a V-4 starting engine.

The Model 830 was built until 1960. During that time, 6,712 were produced. This tractor is the first production model, serial number 830000, constructed on August 4, 1958. The Kellers purchased it from a well-known collector in Iowa named Martha who would tour the collector's circuit on the machine. The deal required months of negotiation, and when the time finally came, Walter and Bruce Keller went to her place in Iowa to pick it up. Walter photographed her and the tractor just before they left, and the photo remains one of his favorites. "This tractor is named 'Martha,'" Walter explains. "It's a tractor she loved."

"Graphics is the visual means of resolving logical problems."

— Jacques Bertin

THE COVER OF THE MAY 1, 1951, *FORBES* MAGAZINE shows Dreyfuss in his brown suit, surrounded by his best-known creations, including the *20th Century Limited*, a Hoover vacuum cleaner, and the Big Ben alarm clock.

Those designs defined Dreyfuss as one of the best industrial designers of the time. Dreyfuss, along with Raymond Loewy, Walter Dorwin Teague, and his former instructor, Norman Bel Geddes, brought style and elegance to daily American life. They also made some of America's largest companies more profitable.

All had talented staffs to execute their visions, but Dreyfuss took a much more hands-on approach than the others. Dreyfuss was not involved much with sales and production, but he was heavily involved in the design and engineering of every product. He personally approved every design generated by his firm, and he would drop in at any hour to give feedback to his people.

In *The Man in the Brown Suit*, author Russell Flinchum recounts a story told to him by HDA designer Jim Conner, who was working on the roll bar for John Deere tractors. Dreyfuss suggested the drawings were too irregular and bristled when Conner suggested they run this by Bill Purcell, another HDA designer. Dreyfuss was incredulous that his authority on design would be questioned.

Dreyfuss kept his client list short so that he could oversee each account personally. He maintained offices in Pasadena, California, and New York City, allowing plenty of face time with clients. A master of quick sketches, Dreyfuss could execute his renderings upside down when meeting with a client seated across a table.

"Our goal has always been to become a member of the client's 'family,' remaining in touch with his problems, co-operating closely on his current merchandise, but also keeping a sharp eye out for future programs," Dreyfuss wrote in *Designing for People*. "We feel that we must be faces and personalities—not merely a voice on the telephone, the signature on a letter, or an initial on a drawing."

The Dreyfuss approach was effective on a number of levels, including compensation. He charged $150 per hour for his services, a figure that shocked even his competitors.

Deere & Company CEO Bill Hewitt embraced Dreyfuss' methods. Due to Hewitt's policy of opening the company's previously closed environment, Dreyfuss was able to work more closely than ever with Deere's engineering and design staff during the creation of the New Generation tractors.

The Model 430 was built between 1958 and 1960. Total production was 14,697. The LP version is a rare machine, with only 68 built.

(PREVIOUS SPREAD) The Model 430 is powered by a 113-ci twin-cylinder engine with a 4.25x4.00 bore and stroke. The gas-engine model makes 27 horsepower at the drawbar.

Converting engines to burn LP fuel was relatively simple process, requiring a different carburetor, an LP converter, and a fuel tank. Henry Dreyfuss would work to cover up the protruding LP tank on New Generation LP tractors.

(OPPOSITE) This Model 430 is equipped with a power-adjustable rear tread width, important for cultivating row crops.

(ABOVE) The dash and controls of the 30 Series were refined using some of the technological advances discovered in the development of the New Generation tractors.

1959 Model 630
Hi-Crop

18

"We can't solve problems by using the same kind of thinking we used when we created them."

— Albert Einstein

THE 1950s FARMER WAS POWER HUNGRY. Hydraulic implements and accessories being developed functioned at higher ground speeds and required more power. Deere & Company had used the two-cylinder engine for nearly five decades, but the design had its limitations. As displacement increased, cylinder volume became inefficient. Larger cylinders also made the engine cases bulky and unwieldy. To continue to produce cutting-edge designs, Deere & Company would need a new, multi-cylinder engine. Protracted debates were held in boardrooms and on production floors. The development costs for retooling the entire line would be astronomical.

Charles Wiman's reign was winding down in the early 1950s and the search for his replacement was on. Some old-line leaders retired, opening the door for younger, more progressive leadership. Mostly, however, the market had spoken: More power was needed. Four- and six-cylinder engines were the best solution.

Not long after the new Model 50 and 60 tractors were introduced as the most advanced tractors ever built, Deere & Company made the decision to create an all-new line of tractors. A handpicked group of about 20 engineers, led by test and development engineer Merlin Hansen, was assigned the task of designing an all-new John Deere tractor.

The engineers would develop the engine in complete secrecy. In early 1953, Deere & Company rented an old grocery store on Falls Avenue in Waterloo to house the group. "The first thing Deere did was put paper over the windows," engineer Ed Fletcher recalled in *Designing the New Generation*, by Merle L. Miller. Locals suspected a new bar was being built and they circulated a petition to protest the establishment. Their assumption was fine with Deere & Company management—the purpose of the facility was not to be public knowledge. Donuts were secretly delivered to the back door to avoid attracting attention. A stern general foreman guarded the property, escorting any interlopers off the property.

In April 1953, key Deere & Company leaders gathered with Dreyfuss and William Purcell to set objectives for the new tractor. The group decided the machine would be a brand-new design. It would be more compact than previous tractors, with an uncluttered underside and streamlined rear end.

The engineering staff asked how much they could depart from history for the new design. Wiman responded that the only absolute rule for the new design was green and yellow paint. In the months that followed, the group considered breaking even that longstanding tradition.

The future of the company rested in the hands of 20 men working long hours behind blacked-out windows in a dumpy, vacant Waterloo grocery store. Deere & Company's next big move would come about in a simple structure—much like the shed in which the first Waterloo Boy was designed.

The Model 630 was available in General Purpose, Standard Tread, and Hi-Crop versions. The General Purpose had four front ends to choose from: a single front wheel, wide-front, dual narrow front, and the dual Roll-O-Matic. The front of this Hi-Crop is clean and presents a timelessly elegant appearance (PREVIOUS SPREAD).

(RIGHT) The 630's 302.9-ci twin-cylinder is fired with an electric starter and produces 48 PTO horsepower. Gasoline, all-fuel, and LP engines were available.

(OPPOSITE) The transmission is a six-speed unit. Top speed is 11.5 miles per hour. Several innovations developed for the New Generation tractors in the mid-1950s were adapted to the 30 Series. One of the easiest to spot is the angled sheet-metal cover at the base of the steering column, which covers the steering shaft.

(FOLLOWING SPREAD) The 630 weighs just more than 6,100 pounds with standard equipment, and could be equipped with a power-adjustable rear tread width as well as cane or rice tires. When Deere & Company engineers set the objectives for the New Generation, they would target the back of the tractor was for simplification and a smoother presentation.

The 630 was produced from 1958 to 1960. Around 18,000 examples were built. This 1959 tractor bears serial number 6315987, making it the last 630 Hi-Crop produced.

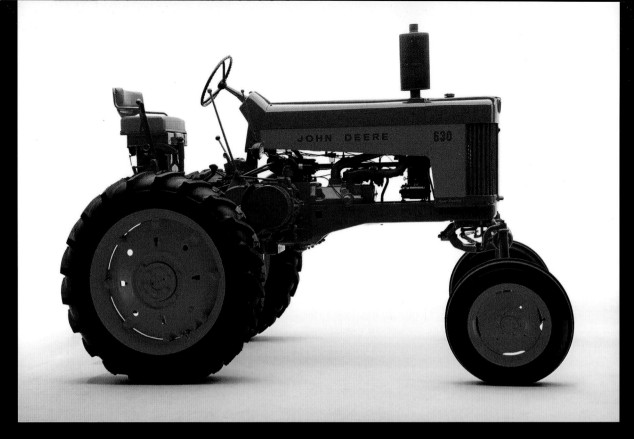

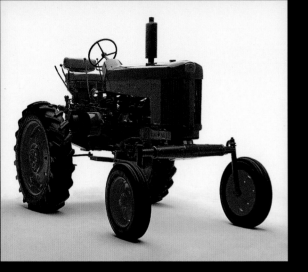

PART 5

THE REVOLUTION

1960 Model 4010

19

"There's a way to do it better— find it."

— Thomas Edison

IN A FORMER WATERLOO GROCERY STORE known to its denizens as the "butcher shop," a group of engineers sequestered away from day-to-day plant operations created the earliest designs for the largest of the all-new John Deere tractors. The team was given broad parameters developed by upper management with input from HDA. Wiman had famously suggested that the only carryover design element from the previous machines should be the green and yellow paint, but on the design board nothing was sacred. Concept drawings depicted yellow tractors with inset stainless steel panels, and even brown tractors.

The most styling attention was given to the hood. The curves were carefully designed to look "right" from any angle. This subtlety was felt to be a crucial way to distinguish the machine in the marketplace. The hood was complemented by seamless surfaces—every screw head and panel junction possible was concealed.

The hydraulic system, transmission, frame, bodywork, hitch, and control systems—nearly every functioning system on the new tractor—were redesigned and improved, but the new engine sitting under that seamless hood was the big story—an engine with more than two cylinders. The butcher boys in Waterloo initially designed a V-6, and according to engineer Merle L. Miller, the author of *Designing the New Generation*, one was built and tested. Eventually, V-4 and V-6 designs were abandoned due to excessive build costs and the extra width required for the V configuration. The engine layout was changed to an inline four- and six-cylinder. This engine design evolved, but the configuration lasted.

The program had begun in 1953 with the intention of having finished machines ready to roll out in 1958. As the designs progressed, it became apparent that redesigning every single system properly would take more time. While the new line was delayed, the 20 Series was replaced by the 30 Series, which incorporated a few of the advances developed by the butcher shop crew.

Finally, in 1960, the new machines were introduced with tremendous fanfare. More than 6,000 people were flown to Dallas, Texas. At noon on August 30, when Tish Hewitt, the wife of Deere leader Bill Hewitt, cut the bow on a giant package near the jewelry counter at the downtown Neiman Marcus department store, the package opened to reveal the new 3010, with diamonds taped to its flanks and a diamond corset on its muffler. The weekend gala was a massive party, capped off with a fireworks display at the Cotton Bowl.

Four models were introduced in Dallas: the 3010 and 4010, as well as the 1010 and 2010. John Deere's New Generation may have arrived glittering in jewels, but the machines were conceived in an old grocery store in Iowa.

John Deere's New Generation tractors were introduced at Deere Day, a gala event in Dallas, Texas, in August 1960. This Model 4010 New Generation is serial number 1000, the first Model 4010 manufactured.

(PREVIOUS SPREAD) John Deere tractors prior to the New Generation placed the operator behind or above the rear wheels. When the front wheel hit a bump, the shock was transmitted to the operator. The New Generation tractors place the operator in front of the back wheels, improving operator comfort.

(ABOVE) One early objective with the New Generation tractors was to keep them compact while dramatically increasing horsepower. The 4010 wheelbase is only about six inches longer than the Model 730, and PTO horsepower increased from 56.7 to 84.0.

The New Generation fuel tank was near the steering column, necessitating purely hydraulic steering. Perfecting the system took inordinate engineering. Plus, test drives were somewhat hazardous, as the early system tended to lock up or drift.

(OPPOSITE) The hydraulics, transmission, brake, and three-point hitch system on the New Generation tractors were new designs, each exhaustively (and secretively) field-tested. The hydraulic system introduced was a closed-center, high-operating-pressure system like those commonly used in 1950s aircraft and machine tool production. The powerful system was not commonly used in agriculture until the New Generation was introduced.

1959 Model 8010
Experimental

20

"Form follows function."

— Henry Dreyfuss

THE ENGINEERING TEAM ASSIGNED TO BUILD the largest addition to the New Generation line started their task by asking farmers what they wanted in a large tractor. In those surveys, farmers responded that they wanted to plow, till, and harrow quickly (at speeds between 4 and 4 1/4 miles per hour) with the largest implements available (which required 5,200–9,500 pounds of drawbar pull). Labor was scarce, so the machine had to be operable by one man.

Farmers worked large plots of land by this time, many of them separated by miles of roads. The tractor had to be road legal, meaning no more than 96 inches wide with a tread weight limited to 18,000 pounds. High transport speeds were also important, along with a fuel supply that allowed 12 hours in the field. Powerful broad-beam lights would allow farmers to work past dark when necessary.

The machine that emerged would become the largest, most powerful John Deere tractor ever built: the 1960 Model 8010. Four-wheel drive supplied the required power and speed. Maximum drawbar power was generated with 67 percent of the weight distributed on the front wheels. Articulation made the tractor maneuverable in fields and on roads.

Walter and Bruce Keller bought and restored the machine you see here. In the summer of 2009, Gerald Mortensen went to a show in Illinois that had several 8010s on display. There, he heard about the Kellers' 8010, and several details sparked his interest. He wanted to come to the Keller farm to see it. When he explained that he was a retired John Deere engineer, the Kellers readily agreed.

At the Kellers', Mortensen carefully examined mounts, gauges, and two loose hydraulic fittings poking from the engine cowl. He concluded that the tractor was not just any 8010, but the prototype that he and his team had built in 1959. The prototype moved on to heavy industrial testing "almost before the paint was dry," according to Mortensen, and was used for implement shows in Arizona and Iowa. A dozer blade and other modifications helped Mortensen identify it at the Keller farm.

Mortensen thought the machine was long gone. "I last saw [it] with the ATECO low-bowl scraper setting in a bone pile back of the Deere foundry [in the] mid-1980s," he recalls. "I thought it was headed for the foundry cupola and didn't expect to see it again."

How the machine made it from the scrapyard to the Iowa dealership is a mystery. Mortensen, for one, is just glad this historic piece of iron found a safe home.

This Model 8010, serial number OW41A, was a prototype used by the John Deere Engineering Research Division to display their brand-new line of New Generation tractors. In fact, this 8010 hauled a gift-wrapped 1010 at the New Generation introduction in Dallas, Texas, in August 1960. The tractor also appeared at farm shows and demonstrations across the United

(PREVIOUS SPREAD) Former Deere engineer Gerald Mortensen identified a number of distinguishing features on this prototype. The hydraulic couplings protruding from the engine bay were used for a dozer-control system built in March 1961. It was the only dozer control system built.

The prototype was converted for industrial

factory. Only 100 production Model 8010s were built, and all 8010s except this example were converted to 8020s by Deere & Company.

(ABOVE) The big machine provides terrific views and comfort for the operator. Henry Dreyfuss and Associates designer Jim Conner worked hard to ensure the lines of the machine reflected its operator-driven engineering.

Operators found ammeters insufficient on a split electrical system. This unique "Bat-O-Meter" (ABOVE) voltmeter was installed on OW41A as a trial and is the predecessor of the modern voltmeter instruments now in common usage. Note the factory inventory tag on the dash.

(OPPOSITE) The bare mounting plate visible on the right fender was for a hand-built rockshaft protractor used to develop the three-point hitch and implements. Note also the two holes in the fender under each rear light. These were drilled at the Deere factory to mount wheel-speed measuring devices.

The 8010 weighs roughly 20,000 pounds and is powered by a General Motors six-cylinder diesel engine that puts out 150 drawbar horsepower. The tractor was also one of the most expensive mass-produced farm tractors ever built, with a retail price in excess of $30,000.

"Tractor collecting is a disease. You catch it just like a cold. You don't know exactly when or where you caught it but then it grows on you and gets worse and worse."

— Walter Keller

ONE DAY, A MAN FROM IOWA whom we'll call Dan phoned Walter Keller. Seems Dan was in California and had located the only gas-powered 4010 Hi-Crop known to exist.

"What if the owner wants $20,000 cash?" Dan asked.

"I'll wire you the money tomorrow," Walter said.

Dan said that wouldn't work. The bank would only let him draw $1,000 per day from a wire. Also, he was headed to a big auction in Indiana. He'd go back to California to get the tractor in three weeks.

"Dan, do it now," Walter said.

"Nope," Dan said. "Get the money together."

Dan suggested that Walter give the money to Dan's daughter, who was on her way home from college and could deliver the cash. Walter agreed to meet her at a filling station in Iowa City. He had a description of her car and a name. That was it.

Walter showed up a bit early and a young woman drove up a few minutes later. She took the cash and drove it 200 miles to her father's house. Dan took the money to California and went to see the man with tractor. There, he showed the man $20,000 in cash.

"I don't want to sell that tractor," the man said irritably. "I just told you that price to get rid of you." Dan thought for a second, then asked the man if he was married. The man responded that he was.

"I tell you what you do," Dan said. "You put this money on the kitchen table where your wife can find it and tomorrow morning she'll tell you what to do with it." He phoned Walter later that evening and told him about leaving the cash with the man.

Walter didn't sleep well that night.

Dan returned the next day and the man agreed to sell the tractor. A week later, the 4010 arrived at the Keller farm.

A few months later, Walter and Dan were talking on the phone.

"By the way," Dan said. "It's white with a lot of chrome."

It took a minute to register with Walter. Then he remembered Dan once telling him that some day he was going to buy Dan a Harley-Davidson. The payday for finding the 4010 turned out to be that "some day."

John Deere made 170 diesel and 11 LP 4010 Hi-Crops. By contrast, they built just one gas-powered unit. This 4010 was that gas model, and it saw years of use on a commercial farm in California.

(PREVIOUS SPREAD and OPPOSITE) This tractor has not been changed since the Kellers acquired it. Even the yellow markings on the side are original. The number 16 was painted on the tractor at the commercial farm where it was used.

(FOLLOWING SPREAD) According to Deere & Company records, this tractor was originally shipped to Appleton, Wisconsin. Eventually it was sent back to the factory, retrofitted with a diesel engine, and shipped to California.

Diesel 4010 serial numbers begin with 22T. This tractor—serial number is 23T 36420—retained the 23T of a gas model after the engine was switched.

Toy manufacturer Ertl used this very machine to create a scale-model tractor. The resulting model had a gas engine and Ertl received numerous complaints from knowledgeable collectors, so they changed it. The original scale model is now highly collectible.

1962 Model 5010

"During the 1940s, product design tended to be not very much more than manipulation of sheet metal, even if its protagonists denied it. Henry Dreyfuss' innovation was to turn it into one of the human sciences."

— Stephen Bayley, *In Good Shape* (1979)

BEFORE WORLD WAR II, designers began to understand that the way in which humans interacted with a machine would impact the machine's function. In the 1930s, scientists began to study body measurements and adapt machines accordingly. During World War II, it was discovered that a significant number of pilots crashed due to confusing control systems. After the war, the defense industry's deep pockets funded studies by teams of engineers, psychologists, industrial designers, and statisticians. Human-factor engineering was born, resulting in machines that interacted more effectively with people.

Henry Dreyfuss' ethics tied neatly into this field. At a time when Brooks Stevens pushed planned obsolescence and Raymond Loewy claimed the most beautiful curve was a rising sales graph, Dreyfuss stated his design goals to be ease of use, safety, efficiency, and comfort.

In the 1950s, Dreyfuss developed standard measurements for people. He gave ranges for everything from finger length to height and dubbed them Joe and Josephine. These two figures became the standards designers would use to create everything from office chairs to steering columns.

Using these standard measurements, Dreyfuss advocated that Deere & Company change its simple seat since he started working with the company in 1937. Deere's organization was so fragmented at that time that the suggestion was ignored. Each department head would have had to sign off on a new seat. So the seats on John Deere tractors continued to be designed in a less-than-scientific manner. One executive even said that seat designs were based on the man with the biggest ass they could find.

The seat would change dramatically beginning in the 1950s with help from Dr. Janet Travell, who had worked with HDA on the seats for the Lockheed Electra and would later become President John F. Kennedy's physician.

Another innovation pioneered on John Deere tractors was the use of universal symbols. Dreyfuss and his wife, Doris Marks Dreyfuss, developed symbols that could be used on equipment and signs around the globe. Some of this work was done at Deere & Company, which was one of the few manufacturers interested in replacing text with symbols. The rabbit and the turtle on the throttle of most John Deere tractors built since the late 1960s are two examples, and are included in Dreyfuss' landmark work, *Symbol Sourcebook*. Published in 1972, the book includes more than 20,000 universal symbols and a multilingual contents page printed in 18 languages, including Chinese and Swahili.

While the symbols and colors on John Deere tractors appear simple and logical today, allowing anyone to intuitively understand the controls' basic functions, the effort to create them was enormous.

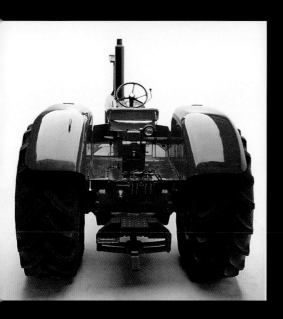

The Model 5010 was produced from 1962 to 1965. This unit is serial number 23T 01000, the first production model built.

(PREVIOUS SPREAD) The Model 5010 uses an eight-speed Synchro-Range transmission. The distinctive prow on New Generation models was designed to give a sense of motion even when the tractor is sitting still.

(OPPOSITE) The Model 5010 provides a front tread of 67 inches.

(RIGHT BOTTOM) The big Model 5010's steering is hydraulic with power assist. The disc brakes are also hydraulically actuated. Its turning radius is just over 12 feet, with the inside brake applied.

(ABOVE) The 5010 produces 105.92 horsepower at the drawbar. It was the largest model John Deere at the time. In 1962 field tests at the Nebraska Tractor Test Laboratory, the 531-ci inline six-cylinder diesel was found to produce 121.12 PTO horsepower.

PART 6

THE TRANSOCEANIC MOVEMENT

"I think that Argentina in particularly will always be our most important foreign market."

— Frank Silloway, Deere & Company board meeting (1923)

ARGENTINA'S *PAMPAS*, 2,000 SQUARE MILES of fertile grasslands, stretch between the soaring 20,000-foot Andes in the west and the lush south Atlantic coastline in the east. These verdant resources attracted European settlers, who poured into the country in the 1870s. Agriculture became one of the nation's most important industries.

Quickly becoming the tenth wealthiest nation in the world, Argentina fed its growth with thousands of imported products. By 1894, its farmers bought more exported American agricultural products than any other country in the world.

Deere & Company machinery was popular there, and 2,194 John Deere tractors sold in Argentina in 1929. When the Argentine economy crashed in 1930, the distributor there struggled to sell its inventory and to pay Deere & Company. As the economy stabilized in the late 1930s, imports picked up a bit.

During World War II, Argentina remained neutral. Postwar anti-Western policies and a slumping economy slowed sales and agricultural growth. When Juan Peron took power in 1946, export policies and developmental priorities shifted. Peron focused on urban rather than agrarian development and aggressively worked to build domestic production and slow imports. Peron's policies improved the country's situation in his first few years of rule—and reduced the import of agricultural equipment.

But Peron became politically oppressive, and the country's inflation rate exploded. He was overthrown in a violent coup in 1955, and Arturo Frondizi eventually took power. Frondizi continued to favor domestic production and encouraged foreign companies to build factories in Argentina. At the same time, Deere & Company President Bill Hewitt was looking to expand into new markets as part of his initiative to make Deere the world's number one tractor manufacturer.

Argentina was a prime agricultural market, and its economy appeared to be stabilizing and growing. Deere & Company decided the time was right to reduce their reliance on their Argentine importer by building machines on South American soil themselves. In September 1957, the company authorized construction of a $3.6 million manufacturing plant in Rosario, Argentina.

Getting the new plant up and running proved problematic. The Argentine government set strict regulations regarding the percentage of the machine that could contain foreign-made parts. When the Rosario plant opened in the late 1950s, initial restrictions were set at 55 percent. The percentage of Argentine-built materials changed over the years, and by 1966, the government mandated that 90 percent of the machines' parts be produced in Argentina. Production costs became excessive, primarily due to these restrictions and labor troubles at the factory, and Deere ended Argentine production in 1971.

This Model 730 was constructed in the United States on August 5, 1958, and shipped, probably in pieces, for assembly at the Deere & Company facility at Rosario, Argentina. When two-cylinder production was halted in the United States, production of the 730 continued in Rosario, and the last 730 built in Argentina was constructed on August 1, 1971. According to records at the Rosario plant, 33,032 Model 730 tractors were built in Argentina.

(LEFT) The Argentine 730s were equipped with diesel engines and electric start. Four versions were built: the Standard, Row Crop (with both a narrow and wide front), and the Hi-Crop.

(FAR RIGHT) The logo on the Argentine Deere models differed from the American-built models.

Argentine Model 730s built after the mid-1960s had nearly every part stamped with "Industria Argentina" or "Industria AG." Rosario is the third-largest city in Argentina. Deere & Company still owns facilities there today.

149

"The whole darn thing looks just too busy—it looks like a Persian carpet."

— Bill Hewitt describing Lanz tractors in a late-1950s letter to Henry Dreyfuss

IN 1859 HEINRICH LANZ FOUNDED A COMPANY importing American agricultural equipment to Germany. The company moved to manufacturing equipment and steam-powered engines, and by 1902 was the largest agricultural company in Germany, employing more than 1,000 workers.

The company's best-known tractor, the Bulldog, was developed by Lanz employee Fritz Huber and introduced in 1921. The simplicity of the tractor's two-stroke, hot-bulb engine and its ability to burn nearly any kind of low-grade fuel was key to the Bulldog's longevity. The machine was produced until 1960, with more than 200,000 units sold.

During World War II, most of Lanz's Mannheim plant was bombed out of existence. After the war, a new, smaller tractor known as the Alldog was rushed into production. Using an engine from a substandard supplier, it was unreliable and caused serious damage to the Lanz reputation.

The Lanz and Deere companies had discussed a purchase since the early 1950s, and by 1956 Deere was increasingly interested in expanding its presence in world markets. Purchasing a German company would give Deere immediate foot in that country. On the surface at least, the deal made sense.

The purchase was completed in 1956. Once they installed new management and began to dig into the details of their new branch, Deere officials discovered the German company was in serious trouble. The tractor product line was too broad and the engines they used were either outmoded or substandard. Company records were poorly kept, and what records there were showed a vast backlog of customer complaints. Deere quickly decided to create a new line using the small utility engines and design from their Dubuque plant. But the new tractors were not built ruggedly enough for European demands, nor did they have the necessary transport road speed.

Beyond the problems of engineering for a foreign market, Deere & Company managers also had serious difficulty adapting to the German culture. The German engineers appeared hidebound and conservative to American management. The fact that German line workers were accustomed to freshly tapped glasses of beer at break time made American management nervous. When the policy was changed so that only small bottles of beer were available, a strike ensued just as the new models were being built. The keg beer was reinstated and remained available on the factory floor for more than 20 years.

The John Deere-Lanz Model 300 and 500 were introduced in the early 1960s. They were handsome, functional machines, but were expensive and somewhat underpowered compared to the competitive tractors built by Massey-Ferguson and Ford.

The Lanz experiment was successful in that it gave Deere & Company a foothold in Europe, but the early results were not what Deere officials were content to accept.

HUILE MOTEUR
ESSO DIOL SDX 30

The John Deere-Lanz Model 3016 is a version of the Lanz Bulldog that was built after Deere & Company purchased the German tractor maker in 1956. One of the first changes that Henry Dreyfuss implemented was to change the Lanz paint scheme from blue to green. Overall, however, his influence in Mannheim was limited, and the Bulldog changed only subtly after the Deere & Company purchase.

The Lanz Bulldog used a two-stroke, hot-... ... a design that features

The mixture is sprayed through ports in the cylinder wall into the cylinder, where it contacts the red-hot portion of the cylinder head.

Starting hot-bulb engines requires the bulb to be heated, which can take several minutes. The engines often started on gasoline and switched over to a low-cost fuel once warm.

The Lanz Bulldog is one of the most prolific models in history. More than 200,000 units were built from 1921 to 1960, and all used this incredibly simple single-cylinder two-stroke ... design.

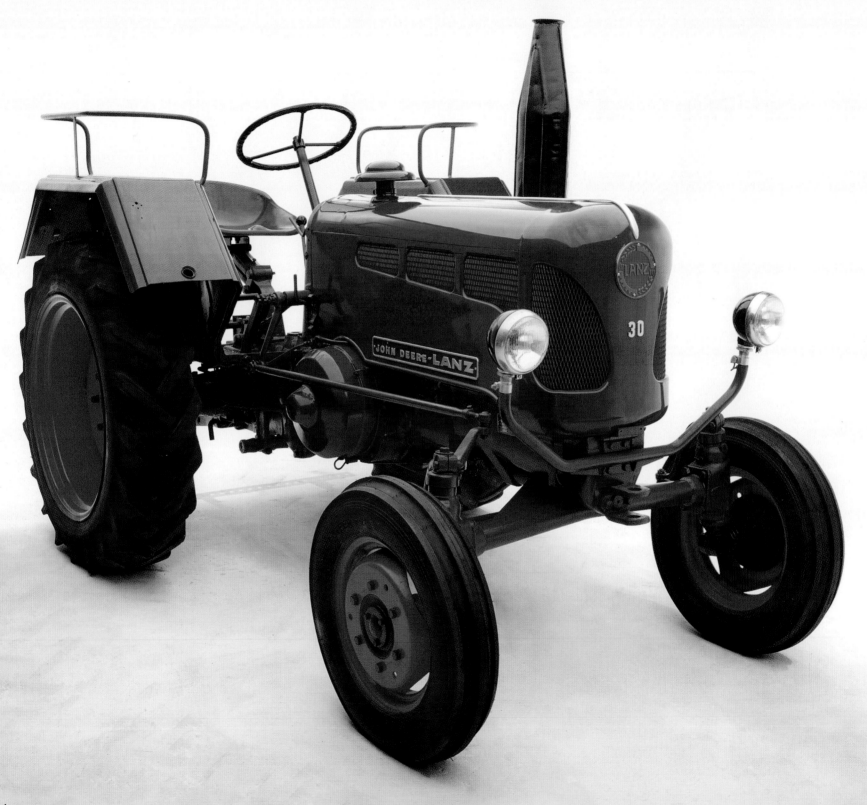

154

155

Model 445S
Argentine Orchard

"Argentina is a country that doesn't wear clothing, but dreams in a tuxedo."

— Julio Cortázar, Argentine writer

WHEN BILL HEWITT TOOK OVER AT DEERE & COMPANY, his goal was to make it the world's top tractor manufacturer. Doing so would require penetration into foreign markets. He admitted to *Forbes* magazine that Deere & Company was behind the curve—competitors had been strong in overseas markets since the dawn of the twentieth century. Deere & Company had no sales offices outside of the United States and Canada.

During the last years of Charles Wiman's management, the company explored a presence in Scotland. Expansion into South America was also considered and rejected. Under Hewitt's direction, the company looked to Mexico and Germany, authorizing an assembly plant in Mexico in 1956, the same year they bought the German company Lanz. A new facility in Rosario, Argentina, was built shortly after that.

As Deere was building in Argentina, Juan Peron encouraged Argentine manufacturers to build their own tractors. The result was the IAME tractor company, which built the Pampa tractor, a virtual copy of the Lanz Bulldog. The machine's simple engine, able to burn almost any fuel—even animal fat—was ideal for the market.

As many as 3,500 blue Pampas were rumored to have been built in the mid-1950s, but the factory lasted only a few years. According to those who have traveled to Argentina in search of John Deere tractors, the Pampa tractors are easy to find. "They are a dime a dozen," one finder named Steve says. Steve has traveled extensively in Argentina and Bolivia, and has been to the archives in Rosario. He finds the machines by wandering.

For a tractor vagabond like Steve, finding desirable machines in strange countries is not overly difficult. The trick is getting them home. "Argentina is full of graft and corruption," he says. "It's not for the meek of heart to bring stuff outside of Argentina." Still, he has managed to ship hundreds of tractors to the United States.

Deere & Company's struggles with Argentina were no less difficult. The government's policies changed constantly, and the company lost money there from the mid-1960s to the early 1970s. Several foreign business leaders were kidnapped and killed by guerillas during the early 1970s, and inflation ran rampant. When terrorist activity abated and the government stabilized in the late 1970s, an agricultural depression hit and interest rates skyrocketed. When import restrictions were reduced, the flood of lower-cost tractors into the country made it difficult for Deere to compete.

International markets present unique challenges. Some, like Argentina, offer a range of problems that are impossible to control. You just have to go with the flow and hope for the best. It's the South American way.

The John Deere 445S is an orchard tractor built in Argentina and powered by a General Motors 2-53 two-stroke diesel engine (PREVIOUS SPREAD). The engines were known to be loud and reasonably powerful. Some were equipped with restrictive mufflers, which reduced power considerably.

The 445S orchard model sheet-metal bodywork is smoother and longer than that on other orchard machines. The styling is also not quite as polished.

(RIGHT) The Model 445 dashboard is quite comparable to that of a Model 430.

This Model 445S came to the Keller collection from an orange grove near Mendoza, Argentina. The machine bears serial number 446003.

John Deere also offered tricycle, vineyard, and "economy" versions of the 445 in Argentina. The latter featured smaller wheels and was shipped without fenders.

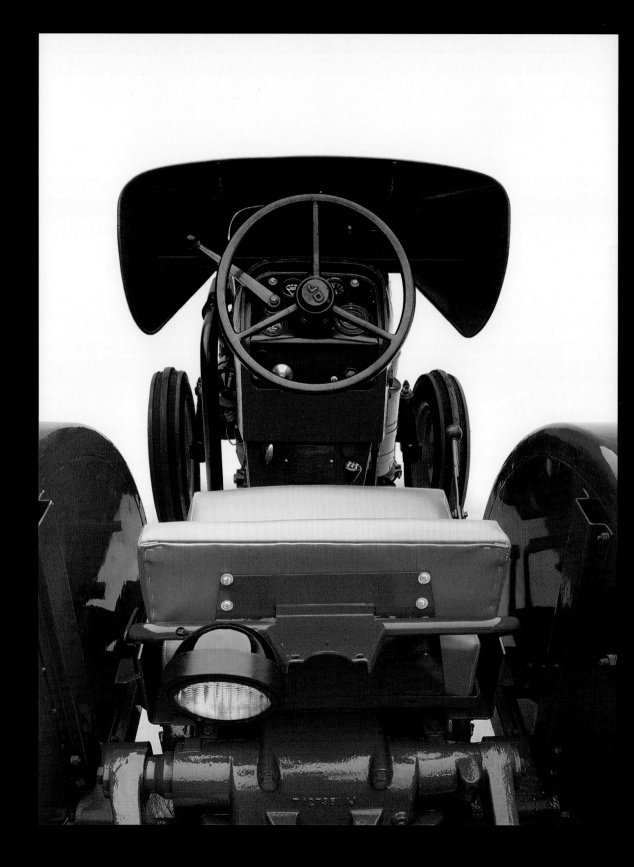

PART 7

THE NEXT GENERATION

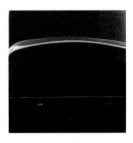

"The difference between a successful person and others is not a lack of strength, not a lack of knowledge, but rather in a lack of will."

—Vince Lombardi

IN 1963, DEERE & COMPANY'S ANNUAL SALES exceeded those of the International Harvester Company (IHC) for the first time in history. John Deere tractors represented 34 percent of all the wheeled tractors sold in the United States. Deere's profitability was also the best in the wheeled-tractor industry. By any measure, the company was the foremost agricultural manufacturer in the world.

Reaching that pinnacle was an impressive accomplishment that resulted from more than a century of growth and development. It is particularly amazing when considering that the company started in the farm tractor industry late and with an established competitor. In the early part of the century, IHC dominated the agricultural industry. When IHC formed in 1902, the company brought most of the major agricultural companies under one banner. The company would eventually face a lawsuit for their monopolistic tendencies, but that wouldn't happen for more than 15 years.

Deere prevailed with the core value of producing great equipment. Cautious with funds and willing to develop their products over long periods, the company remained a steadfast part of the industry even as IHC dominated through consolidation and Ford threw cash and innovation into the fray.

Deere's competition stumbled in the 1950s, at the end of the era when tractors sold at the fastest rate they ever had and ever would. In the late 1940s and 1950s, the postwar economy boomed and farms turned to power in massive volumes. Factories built more than 1,000 tractors per day, and sales soared.

Ford entered the 1950s with a new transmission design. They rushed it into production before it was ready, and their tractors took a terrible beating in reputation and sales. The same happened to IHC when they rushed their high-powered new 560 into production with an old transmission design. That machine put a dent in their reputation and cost millions in a factory recall of epic proportions.

But the problems at IHC went beyond the 560. They overextended themselves, developing lines of appliances and industrial equipment. Overall, their tractor line was still high quality, but they lagged behind John Deere, and their debt load became excessive.

Deere maintained its tradition of long development cycles and responsible investment. The New Generation tractors were built in secrecy and the executives at Deere avoided the temptation of rushing them to market. One wonders what would have become of the company if they had stuck to their original rollout date of 1958 for the new line.

Only 11 examples of the 1963 Model 3020 were built. This is serial number 11T 54539, the first of those 11.

(PREVIOUS SPREAD) Protruding LP tanks were one of Henry Dreyfuss' pet peeves. He advocated a smooth hood design for the first New Generation tractors. With the Model 3020 LP, however, Deere & Company engineers could not find a way to conceal a tank large enough to fuel a day's work. In this case, Dreyfuss'

The 227-ci inline four-cylinder LP engine—a larger-bore, upgraded version of the four-cylinder used to power the 3010—produces 64 PTO horsepower, 56 at the drawbar.

(OPPOSITE RIGHT) The clean and simple cockpit is the result of years of engineering, and the steering system is entirely hydraulic. The two green knobs below the steering wheel are LP gas valves, while the Hi-Crop's rear axle design increases ground clearance in the rear of

(FOLLOWING SPREAD) The hood developed for the New Generation is reinforced in the front, providing better support for front loaders as well as better crash protection. The seats of the New Generation tractors were a vast improvement over the previous platforms. Adjustable and comfortable, they accommodate a wide range of body types and sizes.

1967 Model 500
Industrial

"Deere men pride themselves on knowing the farmer's wants . . . they accord him the respect which city dwellers do not always give."

— *Forbes* (1963)

DEERE'S INDUSTRIAL LINE DATES BACK to the Model D, and over the years thousands of John Deere tractors were built and sold in a variety of colors to work in factories, the military, and other non-farm enterprises.

Early John Deere industrial models (AI, BI, and DI) were sold with limited success. This makes them rare and highly sought after by collectors today, but it didn't earn much favor with management.

Deere & Company continued to sell industrial tractors throughout the 1930s and 1940s. The industrial version of the Model L sold well, as the small machine was well-suited to work on factory floors.

As demand grew, Deere & Company created a separate division in 1957 to build industrial equipment and launched their new product line that same year in Chicago. The Model 64 all-hydraulic bulldozer came out in 1958. In 1959, the industrial line accounted for $48.2 million in gross sales. As the line increased, sales did the same. By 1969, industrial sales at Deere & Company totaled more than $217 million.

The first New Generation versions of the industrial tractors were simply dubbed 1010 industrial, 2010 industrial, and so on. Later models, however, were given a unique nomenclature. The industrial version of the 1020 was known as the 300, the 2020 was the 400, the 3020 was the 500, and the 4020 was the 600. The 5020 was also sold as an industrial model, dubbed the 700.

172

The Model 500 is the industrial version of the Model 3020. The redesigned cowl and hood give it a powerful stance. This 1967 Model 500 bears serial number 100867 and was painted orange at the factory.

(OPPOSITE) A 12-volt electrical system was developed for the New Generation tractors. The starter on the diesel tractors is 24 volts; two

(ABOVE LEFT) The near-seamless lines on the New Generation tractors provide a clear view ahead, and the eight-speed PowerShift transmission was state of the art in the mid-1960s.

(ABOVE RIGHT) The closed-center hydraulic system developed for the New Generation tractors provides power to multiple systems.

means that older hydraulic equipment does not function well with it. The braking system on New Generation tractors is an enclosed oil-bathed disc system. These hydraulic brakes represented large improvements in braking power and longevity, though the hydraulic system in the New Generation tractors required an entirely new type of oil, developed by the

"A tramp, a gentleman, a poet, a dreamer . . . always hopeful of romance and adventure."

— Charlie Chaplin

EXTRAORDINARY EFFORT TRANSFORMED THE 2020 into an orchard tractor. The same can be said of Walter Keller's acquisitions of the rare example shown here.

The machine is a bit of a Frankentractor, the creation of an engineering team working midnight magic to get the operator down low beneath the orchard branches. The entire operator's platform was relocated behind the transmission and differential housing; the seat, steering mechanism, and all control levers had to be stretched and reconfigured.

The result is vaguely industrial in appearance—and a bear to operate. The levers are not well marked, and understanding which gear the machine is in can be tricky. In addition, the clutch is hand-operated. As any early two-cylinder pilot will report, driving a hand-clutched tractor is no walk in the park.

Walter Keller was romanced by this machine when a friend called to tell him about a tractor in Michigan that he had been trying to buy it for a while. Every time he talked to the owner, the price went up, so the friend turned the deal over to Walter and gave him the telephone number of the owner, Evelyn, a single woman living in Massachusetts. They spoke, and she was reluctant to name a price. She did, however, agree to send information about the tractor to Walter.

Evelyn's father had been the original owner, and he had recorded nearly every purchase, oil change, and backfire in the machine's life. "If he bought a spark plug, he wrote down what brand, what he paid for it—everything," Walter says.

The mail continued to stream in from the widow, but she still wasn't willing to name a price. After some time, Evelyn placed a call to the people at *Two-Cylinder* magazine. She was told the tractor was worth $40,000.

She put an advertisement in the magazine, but the next issue wouldn't come out for months. While she waited for the ad to run, Walter continued to romance the deal. "I tried to talk to her and make a deal. We went back and forth almost every week, sometimes a couple times a week," Walter recalls.

The ad eventually came out in *Two-Cylinder*, followed by a second ad. No sales resulted, and Evelyn and Walter continued to correspond. One day, a letter arrived containing the words Walter had hoped to read: "I'll call you and make a deal," Evelyn wrote.

Walter drove to Michigan to pick up the tractor, and to finally meet his pen pal. The deal went as planned and the 2020 was loaded up and brought to Wisconsin.

The 2020 remains in one of Walter's sheds in its original glory, referred to now as "Evelyn's Tractor."

The 2020 orchard model with a gas engine is a rare machine—only 11 were built. This is serial number 84497, which makes it a 1969 model.

The 2020 was built from 1965 to 1971. Inline four-cylinder diesel and gas versions were available. The gasoline-engined Model 2020 produces 53.9 PTO horsepower and 43.94 drawbar horsepower.

(OPPOSITE) To make an orchard tractor, the rear controls had to be relocated, which required extensive engineering. The transmission on the 2020 is an eight-speed Power-Shift unit, and the hand-operated clutch was a convenient solution. It's also popular with orchard growers, who can walk next to the machine while operating it as the extensive fenders and shields push orchard branches aside.

"Deere & Company leads competition in the United States; however, competition is ahead of us in the foreign markets."

— Bill Hewitt, Deere & Company board meeting (September 1960)

IN THE EARLY 1960s, DEERE & COMPANY INVESTED billions into purchasing and establishing plants around the globe. To maximize the advantage of these locations, the company needed common tooling and parts. Harold Brock was tapped to head the engineering team. A former Ford sales manager, Brock had extensive experience with the Ford N series tractors, a platform that was similar in size and configuration to the tractor Deere needed to sell abroad and at home. When the time came to create a small tractor that could compete in the international market, Brock was a logical choice.

The basic parameters for the new machine were laid out in September 1960. It needed to be a general-purpose tractor with a low profile, with an assortment of models ranging from roughly 20 to 50 PTO horsepower. The machine needed to be easily configured to different markets and use standardized components.

The company used two platforms as starting points. One was the existing 1010 and 2010 made in Dubuque; the other was the small Lanz tractor built in Mannheim, Germany.

Brock assembled a team of Deere engineers from Dubuque, Mannheim, and France. "Each had their own idea of what a tractor should be," Brock said. "The German and the French wanted different speed options. Most people [in Europe] live in the city and go out to the farm in the country."

In the past, drawings had been converted from metric to standard or vice versa. Conversions were invariably rounded off, resulting in parts that didn't fit. This team developed a blueprint that used both metric and U.S. measurements, and employed symbols rather than words. The system became an industry standard.

By 1965, the tractors were ready for production. Sorting out where the machines would be built was almost as difficult as designing the tractors. Tariffs, shipping, and customs had to be considered for each country that would build parts. In the end, manufacture of the machines took place primarily in Dubuque and Mannheim. Other components were built at plants around the world.

Three different models were sold in Europe: the 32-horsepower 310, the 40-horsepower 510, and the 50-horsepower 710. The worldwide tractors gave Deere a better product for Europe, and tremendously valuable experience navigating world markets. However, the machines *didn't* give Deere a large market share in Europe.

In the United States, two new models emerged as the domestic versions of the worldwide tractor: the 1020 and 2020. At home, Deere & Company was settling into its role as a market leader. The rest of the world would have to wait.

Introduced in 1965 and produced until 1973, the Model 1020 was designed to meet the needs of small farms worldwide. This 1969 1020 vineyard model is narrower than a standard 1020. It also has a hard nose and lights mounted beside the engine instead of on the fenders.

(ABOVE) The 1020 is powered by a 152-ci three-cylinder diesel engine that produces 34.5 PTO horsepower. It weighs 4,870 pounds without wheel ballast. The weight is distributed heavily to the rear (LEFT).

(OPPOSITE) To avoid translations, the controls of worldwide tractors carried symbols. Dreyfuss played a key role in their development.

The transmission offers eight forward and four reverse speeds. High transport speeds were vital to the European market.

1970 Model 4520
Diesel AWD

"Farmers are no longer hicks,

and neither are we."

— Bill Hewitt, *Forbes* (1963)

EVERY DAY BILL HEWITT COMMUTED FROM HIS HOME in Rock Island, Iowa, to Deere & Company in Moline, Illinois. The 10-minute drive came to a close as he drove his Jaguar Mark X across the glass-enclosed bridge leading to Deere's corporate headquarters.

The complex was designed by famed architect Eero Saarinen, who also designed buildings for IBM, General Motors, and CBS, as well as the Gateway Arch in St. Louis. Completed in June 1964, the pillars on the Deere building were finished in structural steel known as Cor-Ten. This material was shiny for a few years, but anodized over time to a dark, rich brown.

The location is determined by tradition. John Deere—the man—built his first plant in Moline when most of the town's business was run in a single mill. He understood the value of being on the banks of the Mississippi River, and the good local supplies of wood and coal.

Hewitt understood tradition. While his leadership transformed Deere & Company more dramatically than even the construction of their palatial headquarters, he also remained true to the ethics of the man who made the plow his sword. Under his leadership, the divided, independent division overlords were forced to bow to leadership's needs while retaining the ability to influence corporate direction.

In a time when their competitors slipped, Deere & Company created the most exciting new line of tractors in history. The company pioneered the development of a rollover protection system, giving the technology they developed away so that it would actually be implemented.

Under Hewitt's leadership, Deere & Company became the world's largest manufacturer of agricultural equipment. By 1970, the company had manufacturing presences in Brazil, China, Soviet Union, South Africa, Iran, Turkey, Australia, and Mexico, to name just a few. More importantly, Hewitt helped the company create the tools it needed to thrive in the tough times ahead.

The John Deere 4520 was built in 1969 and 1970. This 1970 example is equipped with rare front-wheel assist and a PowerShift transmission. The 4520 listed at $11,600. Roughly 7,800 units were sold.

(PREVIOUS SPREAD) The 4520 was powered by a turbocharged six-cylinder diesel engine with 120 PTO horsepower. This example is the first production turbocharged John Deere tractor.

(ABOVE) The 4520 could be equipped with a cab or rollover protection system. Deere & Company spent years developing state-of-the-art protection for the driver.

PHOTOGRAPHIC NOTES

This book was created due to a perfect storm of factors. The Keller collection was selected as it offers access to an amazing collection of significant John Deere tractors. Walter and Bruce Keller also have a shed large enough to build a portable studio inside of it. Bruce agreed in November 2009 to tackle the task of constructing a studio at his place. After walking around the complex and picking out the machines to be photographed, we carefully measured the largest (the 8010), which is 11 feet high at the top of the stack and 18 feet long.

In order to photograph that machine, the studio needed to be 20 feet wide, 25 feet long, and 15 feet high. Bruce and I settled on a 20x30x16-foot design—better too big than too small.

Equipment was ordered and shipped. The crew painted the floor with special non-reflective high-durability paint. Three men were hired to wash, move, and detail tractors, along with an editorial assistant and a video-studio assistant. On May 13, 2010, seven of us went to work building the studio.

The lighting was one of the keys to the success of this operation. Once it was determined that the best way to light these machines was with direct, even light from overhead, the 10x20-foot Chimera F2 lightbox was the only viable choice.

The Chimera is easily transportable and folds down into three large duffel bags. Once assembled, it is light enough to suspend from the ceiling and provides absolutely stunning light. With a set of Speedotron 4803 power supplies and heads, I was able to shoot at F16 at 1/200th for the entire shoot—even with the lightbox raised 12 feet above the floor. I was able to easily shoot the detail photos without my tripod, saving time. Though the light required tinkering with large bounce cards, the shoot would not have worked as well as it did without the lightbox.

The camera was a Canon 1DS Mark III. This book is a large format, and the 21 megapixels gave the images exceptional clarity. Also, the Mark III's Live View feature allowed me to control it with my laptop computer. As shots were fired, they appeared on the screen. This allowed me to verify light settings quickly and efficiently. It also made me an unrepentant computer-controlled DSLR addict.

The Speedotron 4803s performed absolutely flawlessly. They fired consistently during 10-hour days. PocketWizard radio controls were used to fire the 4803s. Speedotron 102 heads also performed admirably.

A Sekonic L-328 light meter was used before most of the shoots, just to verify all the heads were flashed. I was terribly concerned that a bulb would burn out and I wouldn't notice until after several shoots were ruined.

We kept a Maxtor 500-gigabyte drive on location for storing photos instantly. Video and audio files were also created to document the shoot; these, too, were loaded onto the drive.

A Sony DM-1 and a wireless microphone handled the audio portions of the shoot. A Sony XDCAM EX and a boom microphone were used to film the key video segments, and a Canon 1DS Mark 1 and Nikon D5000 were used to photograph the set construction.

(LEFT) The crew on the set included, from left, Josh Kufal, Bruce Keller, Joseph Holschuh, Tom Gerhartz, Marv Bohrtz, Mike Majeski, Walter Keller, and Lee Klancher.

(MIDDLE LEFT) The Chimera F2 lightbox is assembled and put in place.

(MIDDLE RIGHT) The Canon 1DS Mark III and MacBook provided instant onscreen views of the images as they were made.

(BOTTOM LEFT) The lightbox provided consistent soft lighting. Even with the largest machines in place, the light metered at f16 at 1/200th and lost only about 3/4 stop from the top of the stack to the floor.

(BOTTOM RIGHT) One of the most difficult parts of studio photography is keeping the floor clean. The entire crew pitched in to scrub throughout the shoot and the floor was repainted. *All Josh Kufal*

ACKNOWLEDGMENTS

First, thanks to Walter and Bruce Keller for having the passion to create this incredible collection and to enjoy sharing it. A special thanks to Bruce, whose construction wizardry, dedication, and leadership made the shoot run smoothly.

To video and photographic assistant Josh Kufal, for his invaluable photo and video knowledge, work ethic, and sense of humor.

To editorial assistant Joseph Holschuh, for his hard work, attention to detail, and willingness to chip in on any task on the set.

To Marv, Tom, and Mike, for all their efforts washing, pushing, polishing, and building on the set.

To Dennis Pernu at Voyageur Press, a dedicated editor and a good friend, who shepherded this project through to completion.

To Joan Hughes for all her support, suggestions, and love.

Thanks are also due to Harold Brock; Gerald Mortensen; Steve; Bob Haight; John Frye; Mark Weaver; Brian Holst; Guy Fay; Sarah Detweiller at the University of Wisconsin–Green Bay; Bill Kapinski at Image Studios; Philip Cousins and Eileen Healy at Chimera; Randy Leffingwell; James F. Bland, Kirk Tuck and the rest of the ASMP crew in Austin; and Michael Dregni, Becky Pagel, LeAnn Kuhlmann, Maurrie Salenger, and Hollie Kilroy at Voyageur Press.

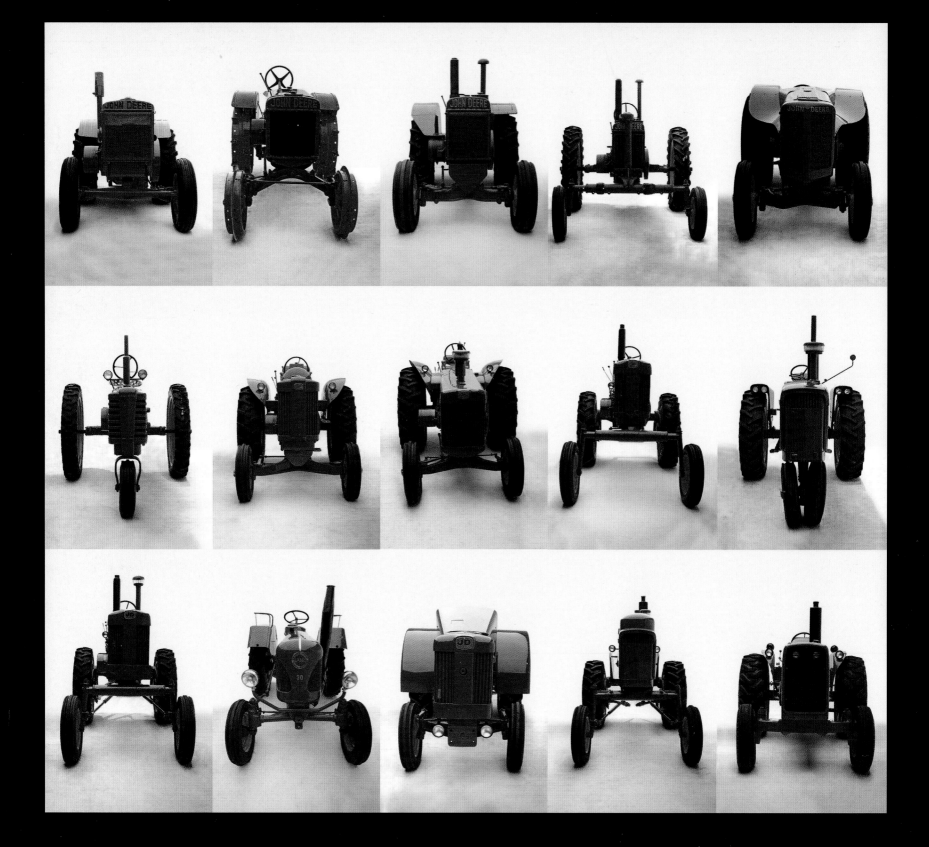